Praise for *Making Every PE Lesson Count*

Making Every PE Lesson Count: Six Principles to Support Great Physical Education Teaching is an insightful, accessible and personal narrative resource for developing and engaged physical educators. This book offers a range of intimate perspectives on how to tackle key considerations in the delivery of high-quality and accessible physical education. It has understanding and progress for learners at its heart – essential for all practitioners to understand and engage with, but also for anyone who may need to know more regarding what physical education is about, beyond sport and physical activity. The book offers comprehensive and practical approaches, with actionable strategies to create engaging and effective learning experiences. Diagrams and pictures provide useful summaries of key information. James Crane has captured the heart and soul of physical education, with a clear and accessible writing style, readers will quickly understand the challenges and rewards of teaching physical education.

**Dr Julia Potter, Head of Physical Education,
University of Chichester**

I love the film *Kes*. This is no *Kes*, but to paraphrase Kevin Keegan, 'I love it.' Why? It's as much about the learning as it is about the movement.

James doesn't sit on the fence, yet he does create a balance – a balance between research and practice. A pracademic, perhaps? He also manages to balance creating opportunities for elite athletes while encouraging all students to develop a love of physical activity.

James has an uncanny ability to draw you into the setting, whether it be the sports hall or the track or field. You can get a real feel for the conversations between the teacher and students.

Whether you're new to the profession of teaching PE and/or sport or a seasoned pro, this book is for you. It's filled with gentle nudges that will enable you to enable your students to succeed.

**Bryn Llewellyn, former school leader and founder of Tagtiv8,
co-author of *How to Move & Learn***

This book is easy to read, written with passion and packed with practical ideas, tips and prompts for reflection. From trainees to experienced PE teachers, all are likely to find something that improves their practice in this book. It is structured so you can dip in and focus on a specific aspect or read it as a whole. Heads of department could easily take this as a template for their team's CPD.

Kevin Lister, Deputy Head Teacher, Stratford upon Avon School, and author of *Teach Like You Imagined It*

Making every
PE
lesson count

*Six principles to support great
physical education teaching*

James Crane

Edited by Shaun Allison and Andy Tharby

Crown House Publishing Limited
www.crownhouse.co.uk

First published by

Crown House Publishing Limited
Crown Buildings, Bancyfelin, Carmarthen, Wales, SA33 5ND, UK
www.crownhouse.co.uk

and

Crown House Publishing Company LLC
PO Box 2223, Williston, VT 05495, USA
www.crownhousepublishing.com

British Library Cataloguing-in-Publication Data

A catalogue entry for this book is available from the British Library.

Print ISBN 978-178583719-7
Mobi ISBN 978-178583725-8
ePub ISBN 978-178583726-5
ePDF ISBN 978-17853727-2

LCCN 2024933119

Printed and bound in the UK by
Gomer Press, Llandysul, Ceredigion

Acknowledgements

This book would not have been possible without the guidance of Shaun Allison and Chris Runeckles. Both have been directors of the Durrington Research School, where I have been fortunate enough to work for the past five years. They have each offered me their unwavering support while challenging me both professionally and personally. They have been superb to work with and consistent in driving forward evidence-informed practice in our region. I am now lucky enough to be able to call them colleagues and friends – thank you both for everything.

This book is a product of my teacher training and time spent working in three excellent PE departments. I want to thank everyone with whom I have come into contact, as those small interactions have been a part of enabling me to write this book. Even my two best friends, Ollie and Jase, despite not working in education, have provided me with insightful perspectives. A special mention must go to the superb Durrington High School PE department; I could not be prouder to be a part of this team. Their professionalism and commitment are integral in nurturing our young people to develop their knowledge, skills, understanding and curiosity in the wide world of sport.

It is the PE teachers working tirelessly in schools up and down the country that are shaping the Alan Shearers and Helen Housbys of tomorrow. You are doing an amazing job in inspiring the young people in your schools, putting them on the path towards a lifelong love of sport and PE. Your passion and dedication are pivotal in supporting each and every child you teach.

I must also take this opportunity to thank Andy Tharby and Shaun Allison for providing me with the opportunity to write this book. Their thought-provoking editing has been a wonderful process for me to go through. I feel lucky enough to work with both of you in my day job, and I am extremely grateful for your support throughout this new endeavour.

My mum and dad have always been my biggest supporters, driving me round the country to play football and offering me insights into wider life lessons. You have always been my greatest supporters and have forever been in my corner, no matter what. I hope this book makes you both proud.

My wife, April, and 5-year-old son, Oscar, have been my rocks while writing this book. Their patience and under-standing have enabled me to have the time and space to talk things through and ensured the process has been a smooth one. Oscar has always been keen to help me write the book, getting his pencils and paper out to sit with me at the dining room table. He has also been more than happy to nip into the garden and play some sport when I need to have a break. April has been the central person in believing in me and always being the voice of reason when I need it most, and all while being pregnant with our second child, a beautiful little girl called Phoebe. I literally could not have done this with-out you. You're amazing. I love you very much.

Contents

Introduction

When people are asked about their favourite subject when they were at school, there seems to be a large swathe that passionately turn to PE, shouting about their love for a specific sport or a teacher who made the subject an enjoyable experience. This is certainly the case for me; I look back fondly on my PE lessons and the impact they had on me as I matured into adulthood.

In the early 2000s, I attended King Richard School in Cyprus. My PE teacher was Mr Lane, and he taught me from Year 9 through to Year 11. I had always enjoyed PE; I played a lot of sport outside of school and relished any opportunity to be physically active, even more so if there was a competitive element. It was Mr Lane who captured this and pushed me to be the best version of myself. His passion, enthusiasm, strong subject knowledge and unwaveringly high expectations of what I could achieve ensured PE and sport would be a huge part of who I am.

PE provides an incredibly unique opportunity for students to flourish: some become professional athletes, others achieve excellent outcomes at GCSE and A level. However, if you ask any PE teacher, their main aim is for all students to leave them once they finish school with a love of physical activity and the lifelong habit of participation – at whatever level of expertise. The benefits on physical, mental and social health are undeniable. The place PE holds in the curriculum is therefore fundamental to society, but it can also be used as a vehicle to promote resilience, determination and perseverance.

Mr Lane found that balance perfectly. He ensured that we all fostered a love of physical activity while developing our understanding of the nuance of a wide range of sports. His drive and love for the subject shone through all aspects of his teaching, but this alone didn't make him a brilliant teacher. His effective practice was built on high expectations and challenge: whatever the activity, his technical language and tactical know-how was never dumbed down, no matter the prior experience of the students. Through clear and well-thought-out explanation, he gave the activity context which helped me feel like an aspiring gymnast when designing my floor routine. The feedback he gave was focused and purposeful, which enabled me to use it to improve my performance. His biggest strength was that he used his questioning to probe me and ensure that I was thinking deeply about my performance, where my knowledge gaps were and what I could do to ensure that I was constantly reflecting, thinking and improving.

Thankfully, when I returned to a school setting as a trainee PE teacher, independent learning and a somewhat whimsical way of teaching was on its way back out. The power of knowledge and high-quality instruction were once again regarded as the cornerstones of the teaching world.[1] What had proved invaluable to me as a student in Mr Lane's class was, in fact, great teaching.

---

1   Robert Coe, Cesare Aloisi, Steve Higgins and Lee Elliot Major, *What Makes Great Teaching? Review of the Underpinning Research* (London: Sutton Trust, 2014). Available at: https://www.suttontrust.com/wp-content/uploads/2014/10/What-Makes-Great-Teaching-REPORT.pdf.

Although this might not be groundbreaking to hear, it does provide reassurances that we have solid foundations behind the choices we make every day in our teaching. This book aims to synthesise the latest research on teaching and learning and present it specifically for PE teachers. There is a huge amount of evidence available, too much for a classroom teacher to be expected to engage with directly. This book does not claim to be an exhaustive review of the educational research; indeed, there will be areas that fall outside of its remit and, as such, will be omitted. However, it does aim to bridge the gap between the world of academic research and PE teaching.

In *Making Every Lesson Count*, Shaun Allison and Andy Tharby describe six pedagogical principles that are the bedrock of great teaching.[2] The first principle, challenge, is the flagship of teaching, ensuring students struggle and having high expectations of what they can do. Only then will they be able to move beyond their existing knowledge and skills. The second principle is explanation, which is the ability to articulate new concepts and ideas. Explanation makes the abstract appear concrete in students' minds, which is no mean feat and rather tricky to do well. The next principle is modelling. This involves physically showing the students how to tackle problems or complex procedures, making the implicit processes we go through as experts explicit to students, in order to support them to apply the same principles, processes and procedures themselves. Students require sufficient time, within set parameters, in order to practise these processes enough to support the retention of the knowledge and skills long term. Practice is the pinnacle of the six principles as it is where the most crucial element of learning comes to the fore: memory. Students need to be aware of where they are, where they are going and how they are going to get there – which is why coiled up with practice

---

2   Shaun Allison and Andy Tharby, *Making Every Lesson Count: Six Principles to Support Great Teaching and Learning* (Carmarthen: Crown House Publishing, 2015).

comes feedback. Without feedback, practice becomes redundant and stagnant. Practice does not make perfect unless feedback is used to guide students and impact their future practice, ensuring that they make progress. The final principle is questioning. This is about the dialogic subtleties we go through in order to support the learning cycle. Questions are used to keep students on track, check their understanding, identify misconceptions and promote deep thinking around a topic or activity. Good PE teaching is littered with all of the principles, not as a checklist or plan as such, but to ensure that teaching is well structured and thought out. The art of the principles is in deploying them to adapt our teaching to ensure that we are navigating the unpredictable, ever-changing landscape of our students.

The six principles are already inherent in the best PE teaching. However, there are a number of challenges for PE teachers to overcome, and it is worth exploring these one at a time.

Sequencing of the Curriculum

Perhaps the biggest battle we have as PE teachers is over the spaces we have available to us throughout the academic year. The sports hall being out of bounds for Year 11 exams, the gym being taken along with the table tennis tables for Year 8 jabs, the main hall being blocked out for three weeks so the school production can rehearse. The list seems to be infinite, but that is only half the battle. Our sequencing issues impact our curriculum offer, our teaching strategies and our assessment criteria, moderation and standardisation. In an ideal world, we would all teach Year 8 badminton at the same time, in the same way in which maths departments tend to teach Year 8 simplifying expressions – for example – in the same block of lessons. It allows for rich departmental discussions, particularly the sharing of common misconceptions and strategies to address them. In PE, this is simply undoable. Most schools have one sports hall and may have up to eight classes on at the same time, creating a physical impossibility for those classes to be taught the same unit of work at the same time. The maturational development students go through from one term to the next is startling. To have a curriculum that is coherent and rigorous, supported with assessment, is hard enough when this challenge isn't there, but, simply put, sequencing all classes on the same topic at the same time is not an option for the vast majority of PE teachers.

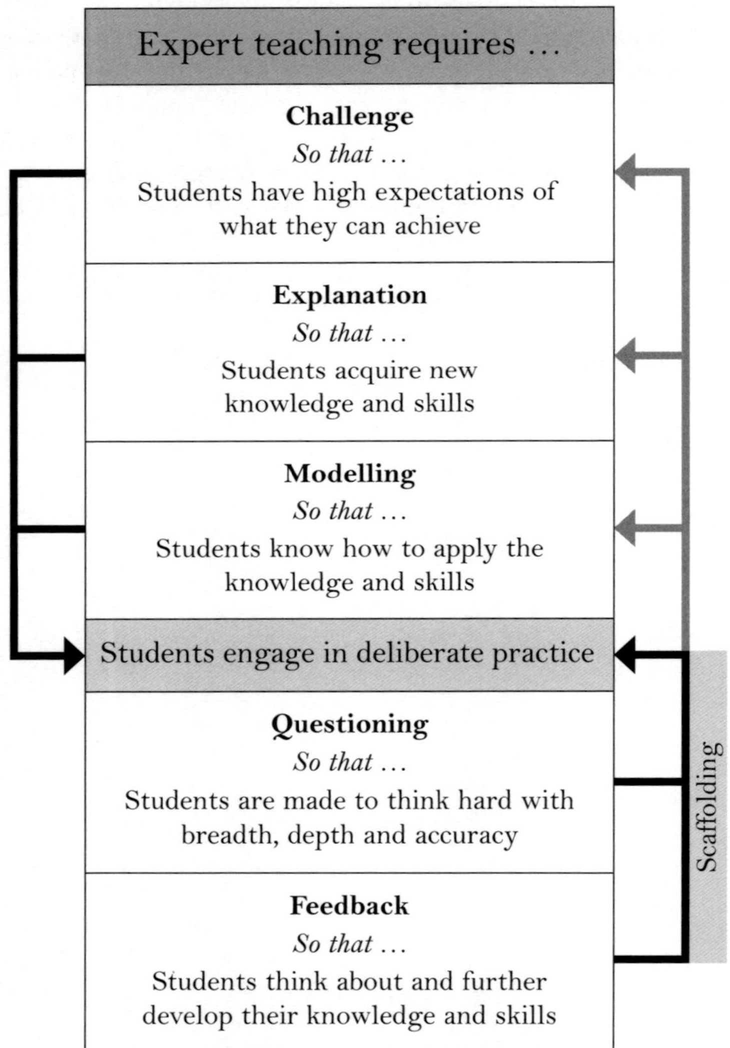

Expert teaching requires ...
Challenge
So that ...
Students have high expectations of what they can achieve
Explanation
So that ...
Students acquire new knowledge and skills
Modelling
So that ...
Students know how to apply the knowledge and skills
Students engage in deliberate practice
Questioning
So that ...
Students are made to think hard with breadth, depth and accuracy
Feedback
So that ...
Students think about and further develop their knowledge and skills
Scaffolding

Breadth vs Depth

The PE curriculum creates a moral dilemma. On one hand there is the important element of students experiencing a wide range of sports, which will support them in finding their love of physical activity and thus promote lifelong participation. The other element is the development of a deep level of understanding of the complexities of fewer sports, coupled with supporting students to excel at GCSE and A level. The question is always hotly discussed among PE teachers: do you have a broad curriculum to foster a love for sport more generally, or do you promote elite sport for all in a deeper-level curriculum? The answer, I suppose, is balance. The aim is to promote both avenues while ensuring that you have high-quality outcomes and create opportunities for students to experience a wide range of activities.

Subject Knowledge

Most UK PE teachers will be expected to teach invasion games, net and wall games, striking and fielding games, outdoor adventurous activities, dance, swimming and water safety, and gymnastics, even though they will have likely specialised in only one of these disciplines during their higher education. Furthermore, during their playing careers, they may have only played one sport to a level which would mean their subject knowledge can be considered expert. The Sutton Trust's 2014 report, *What Makes Great Teaching?*, lists subject knowledge as an imperative characteristic of great teaching.[3] This presents a very real problem for PE teachers. How can the level of challenge be appropriate for all students, through effective questioning and modelling, when we are teaching outside of our specialism? Therefore,

---

3   Coe et al., *What Makes Great Teaching?*, p. 19.

the following limitations are likely to present an issue unless we act to address them:

♦ Subject knowledge will be less robust.

♦ The ability to identify and address misconceptions will be limited.

♦ The teacher will bring their own misconceptions into play.

♦ There will be less challenge through effective questioning and modelling.

♦ Understanding of how to support students in their decision making will be limited.

The Relationship Between Practical and Theory

As GCSE and A level PE have become more heavily weighted on theory, and theory content and assessment complexity has increased, more and more schools are beginning to alter their curriculum, affording more hours to theory at the expense of practical lessons. There is a finite number of hours in the day and, with all subjects becoming more content heavy, the balance between practical and theory lessons in PE is a prevalent one. Some schools have introduced a theory element into their Year 9 curriculum or have moved to more theory lessons and fewer practical lessons at Key Stage 4 and 5. This discussion point comes back to moral purpose and how schools keep physical education physical in an ever-changing environment. Of course, how we utilise our extracurricular programme is pivotal to students' development. This book will explore how PE teachers can ensure a focus on physical activity while supporting theory concepts through a curriculum built on high expectations and challenge for all students.

Knowledge of Students

The students we teach will have a vast range of sporting backgrounds and differing knowledge in both theory and practical settings. PE teachers need to be able to identify students' prior capabilities and understanding, then carefully stretch and challenge each of them through effective delivery, questioning and feedback. How do you scaffold questioning to ensure that students feel confident enough to answer while also being sufficiently challenged to think deeply? What is the most effective way to give students feedback that is both purposeful and manageable?

While the six pedagogical principles provide an overarching framework for great teaching, great teachers need to be great at teaching their subject. This means that they must understand the challenges of implementing these principles within the context of their specialism. Only then can they develop their pedagogy, use it to overcome these challenges, and become expert subject teachers. That is the purpose of this book: to help all PE teachers reflect on the challenges of implementing the six pedagogical principles in their own settings, and provide them with evidence-informed strategies that they can try out to make every PE lesson count.

In each chapter, you will find a number of practical teaching strategies designed to bring the six principles to life, followed by some reflective questions. Nevertheless, all schools are different, so it is up to you to refine them to suit your classes and activities. After all, you are the expert in your setting and on your students.

Comfort zone	Struggle zone	Panic zone
Low challenge. Low stress. Limited thinking. Limited learning.	High challenge. Low stress. Thinking required. Effective learning.	Very high challenge. High stress. Cognitive overload. Limited learning.

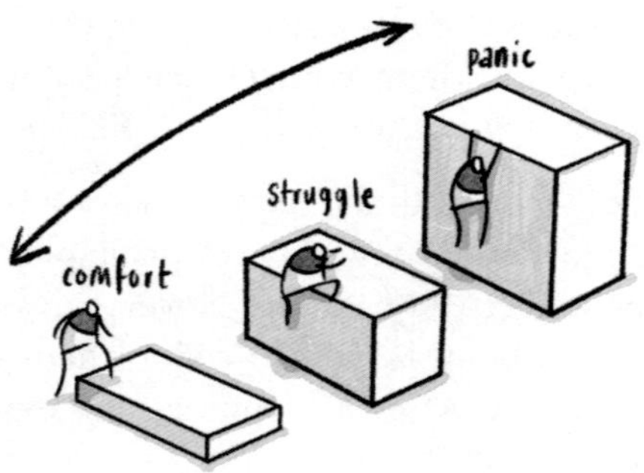

Chapter 1
Challenge

Challenge can be described as the provision of difficult work that causes students to think deeply and engage in healthy struggle. This can be problematic for all teachers, but there are unique issues that make this especially difficult for PE teachers. During any one lesson, PE teachers will have up to 32 students in their teaching space, all of whom will have different prior knowledge of the activity, different levels of tactical understanding, varying degrees of physical capabilities and understanding of the key principles within that activity and different misconceptions. Alongside this, their level of interest in the sport or even the specific activity will vary widely, ranging from the super-keen county-level athlete, who has always been enthralled by sport, to the surly teenager who appears to have a complete aversion to the set task, almost to the point of hatred. It is our job to synthesise all of this information and then push each student to keep them in the sweet spot of the struggle zone.

Challenge is slightly different from the other five principles. For example, questioning, explanation and modelling are clear tangible elements of a lesson that are direct in their purpose, and it is clear when the teacher is modelling, questioning or explaining. While there are specific teaching strategies that can be employed to ensure that challenge is appropriate for all the students we teach, the principle is more about an approach to teaching. Challenge is a long-term venture and should run through everything we do as PE teachers – like Newcastle United runs through Alan Shearer. It's about the culture we create in our teaching space and the expectations we have of the students we teach. The objective is always to try to keep students in the struggle zone, as shown in the figure on page 10. This requires students to be thinking hard enough to support learning, but not be so stretched that they reach cognitive overload and slip into the panic zone, where learning will be limited. At the other end of the spectrum, the work should not be too easy, resulting in students remaining in the comfort zone.

The best PE teachers create this culture by getting to know the students they teach, taking a genuine interest in their progress, making them believe that they can achieve beyond their own expectations and then supporting them – through the other five principles – to meet these expectations. Their lessons are places of intrigue, warmth and safe challenge, where students feel secure enough to push and test their own thinking.

So, let's explore some strategies that we can put into place to grow this culture.

Challenge Strategies

1. Curriculum

The first thing we should endeavour to do, as secondary PE teachers, is ensure that we have a challenging and interesting curriculum. Largely due to the limitations surrounding space and the added complexities when selecting activities, such as time of year, teacher specialism and available equipment or facilities, curriculum is a contentious issue in PE. When thinking about the construction of the curriculum, we should always consider: is it giving students enough opportunities to make informed decisions about maintaining a healthy, active lifestyle? Is there enough depth so that students can understand and apply their knowledge of rules and strategies while developing their motor competence? This coupled up with identifying which sports to teach and how to sequence them – and justifying why they should be taught – proves to be a complex problem.

Although there is no silver bullet when it comes to curriculum design, most schools have some common activities that feature in Years 7, 8 and 9. By 'activities' here, we mean sports, drills, exercises, practices, etc. These activities roughly follow a familiar model of learning the key skills and techniques in Year 7, applying and refining them in Year 8 and then exploring them in their full context in Year 9. This does not mean that a full game will not be covered until Year 9, but that the focus of that full game in Year 7 or 8 will be on skill development. For example, in football you may learn the technique of short passing in Year 7. As you move into Year 8, you may learn how and when to use different types of passes under pressure. The Year 9 development may be how to use variations of passing effectively in a game situation. Although this creates an element of continuity – motor competence and understanding and knowledge of rules and strategies are expected to improve over time – it doesn't create a coherent curriculum. The challenge of curriculum planning is having coherence within revisited activities (drills, strategies, techniques, etc.) across terms or year groups but also between different sports. My colleague, Ryan De Gruchy, did this in a highly effective way. He explains the process as follows:

♦ *First of all, I identified the common threads running through all activities taught in Key Stage 3 as: performance, sporting values and key knowledge.*

♦ *I split this further into the composite parts of each thread. Performance is made up of skills and techniques, decision making and fitness. Values is made up of leadership, attitude and teamwork. Key knowledge is made up of tier 3 terminology (low-frequency subject-specific words), sporting knowledge and analysis. The performance threads are very dependent on the practical activity and, in essence, are about improving the learner as a performer in that activity. However, sporting values and key knowledge are threads that run through the curriculum chronologically regardless of practical activity.*

♦ *These threads were then intertwined into the curriculum and explicitly taught to students across all practical activities. For example, the thread of teamwork starts in Year 7 with developing communication and listening skills in term 1, moving on to cooperation and problem solving as a team in term 2, before using teamwork skills to tackle complex problems in term 3.*

♦ *The curriculum threads were then directly and explicitly embedded into the assessment model used at Key Stage 3.*

We should scale up our Key Stage 3 curriculum to ensure students are being exposed to challenging materials. In table tennis, for example, instead of teaching the forehand and backhand push shots as standalone components, why not teach students about generating topspin, backspin or sidespin to put pressure on their opponents. Provided we scaffold their learning carefully, most students will rise to the challenge. This could be through the physical development of the shot for your practically able players. However, even if they can't execute it yet, everyone can develop their understanding of how to use spin to put their opponents under pressure, when to use the variations during game play and how to make decisions during the game. Some may need more time to perfect the push shot, but they can be learning about the skill and benefiting from repeated exposure to it in the meantime.

When asked to describe what she had been learning about in PE, Lucia, a Year 8 student at Durrington High School, responded:

Miss Cann has been teaching us table tennis and the use of topspin on the forehand side to try and put pressure on our opponents during games. When I was playing a game, my opponent was just pushing the ball over the net, so I was able to use topspin to generate more speed, giving them less time to react. I was also able to move them around the table until I could use the topspin shot from a cross-court rally into a down-the-line winner.

The student response demonstrates an understanding of how to outwit their opponent but also shows knowledge of how to make effective decisions in real time. Had the school not reviewed the Key Stage 3 curriculum and scaled up the content, this knowledge and performance level would not have been evident. The important thing here is that students are being exposed to more demanding concepts.

This should also be the case during Key Stage 4. By exposing students to material that is just beyond the expected level of the GCSE specification, this hardest content will make what they have to remember for their exams seem easier by comparison.

John Fuller, a deputy head teacher and PE teacher at Durrington High School, and Tom Pickford, director of PE and sport, both do this at specific points in the curriculum. John outlines a specific point in the AQA GCSE PE Paper 2 unit on arousal:

When teaching arousal and the inverted U theory, to show greater breadth around arousal theorem we discuss both the drive and the catastrophe theory. This ensures that students are aware of the wider discussion around arousal, allowing them to make more informed decisions when it comes to the Paper 2 exam. The discussion sparks interest but also allows me to question the deeper topic of sports psychology and how that directly impacts sports performers, such as Roberto Baggio at Italia '90.

Tom has also amended the Paper 1 curriculum to allow for more content beyond GCSE to be embedded and discussed:

One of the questions I used to get asked by my GCSE students was: 'If anaerobic respiration is 80–90% of maximum heart rate, what is 90–100%?' This has led to me tweaking the curriculum to delve deeper into energy systems and move on beyond aerobic and anaerobic. We now include the Krebs cycle, the lactic acid system (rapid glycolysis) and creatine phosphate system. This not only supports students with their understanding of their GCSE content but also leads to wider discussions around A level PE and the different sports that involve activating the anaerobic system.

2. PE Talk

Marc Rowland says that every moment in school needs to be a language development and comprehension moment.

Language is the key to success in accessing the curriculum, participating in lessons and developing background knowledge that binds learning together. Oral language, especially, is a key indicator for future academic success.[1] This is the case for all subject areas, including PE. Particularly significant is vocabulary and the three different vocabulary tiers, as outlined by Dr Isabel Beck et al.:[2]

- Tier 1 – high-use words. These can include objects and adjectives. These tend not be taught in schools as they are usually learnt pre school (e.g. window, car).

- Tier 2 – cross-curricular and are usually descriptive. These words can often be explained using easier and more familiar words, commonly tier 1 words – for example, 'excessive' is a more mature way of describing more than is necessary. These are words that are useful across subjects and in various situations (e.g. evaluate, service, environment, flexibility). Students are likely to come across these words through exposure to written texts and are unlikely to come across them in day-to-day discussion.

- Tier 3 – low-repetition words. These are subject-specific words and are not encountered a great deal in everyday language; when they are, they tend to be particular to a subject (e.g. respiration, cardiovascular, vasodilation, sagittal). If students don't understand the meaning of the words, and so can't use them appropriately, their academic achievement may be limited.

Language has implications for PE teachers. Firstly, we need to explicitly teach the subtle differences in the meaning of a tier 2 word in a PE context compared to its use elsewhere. Students quite often understand the term 'environment' to mean the natural world around us (e.g. we should recycle as it is good for the environment). In the context of PE, it has

---

1   Marc Rowland (ed.), *Addressing Educational Disadvantage in Schools and Colleges: The Essex Way* (Woodbridge: John Catt, 2021), p. 67–68.
2   Isabel L. Beck, Margaret G. McKeown and Linda Kucan, *Bringing Words to Life: Robust Vocabulary Instruction* (New York: Guilford Press, 2002).

a more specific meaning. It refers to the conditions of a specific activity. The definition of fitness is: 'the ability to meet or cope with the demands of the environment'. The demands of the environment in football would be to run, pass, dribble, tackle and shoot for 90 minutes in a 100m by 55m rectangle. Secondly, we need to expose students to tier 3 PE vocabulary on a regular basis. It is imperative that we don't dumb down our language (e.g. 'He is really good at the marathon as he can work really hard without getting tired quickly.'). We need to expose students to and teach them the correct meaning and use of PE vocabulary (e.g. 'He is really good at the marathon as he has excellent cardiovascular endurance and this delays the onset of fatigue.'). This tier 3 vocabulary will need to be taught and we need to insist on students using it. Marc Rowland suggests the following approaches to deepening knowledge through robust vocabulary instruction:[3]

- Explaining the meanings of words in everyday, student-friendly language, rather than using dictionary definitions.

- Providing numerous contexts to show how a word can be used.

- Getting students to interact and connect with word meanings.

- Getting students to act out or engage with the meanings of words in a variety of ways.

- Providing interesting and concrete examples of the use of new words.

- Providing lots of opportunities for students to use new words.

My colleagues, Louise Wallis-Tayler and Alex Cann, explain how they have looked at GCSE tier 3 terminology with a view to embedding it into the Key Stage 3 curriculum. This is done in the same way as we would start to drip-feed GCSE assessment criteria into Year 9 to raise the challenge.

3　Rowland, *Addressing Educational Disadvantage in Schools and Colleges*, p. 68.

Firstly, we looked at the GCSE topics that students typically struggled with, following discussions with the teachers and the students. This boiled down to, in most cases, a lack of understanding of the tier 3 terminology. So, we thought a way to raise the challenge of the Key Stage 3 curriculum while supporting the transition into GCSE would be to try to introduce the most common 30 words that our students struggled with during Key Stage 4 throughout Key Stage 3. This is done in line with the spaced practice model and through teacher explanation, questioning and modelling. We didn't want to take away from practical lesson time, so we wanted this to support the teaching and not be a bolt-on [an example of how this looks is below]. We monitored this through drop-ins and targeted questioning of students around their understanding of the word in the context of a range of activities and, at times, the etymology of the word. The same vocabulary was explored in Year 7, 8 and 9 and built upon each time. In Year 7, students identify and define the term. In Year 8, they begin to apply it to a variety of sports or activities. Finally, in Year 9, they analyse and evaluate the word.

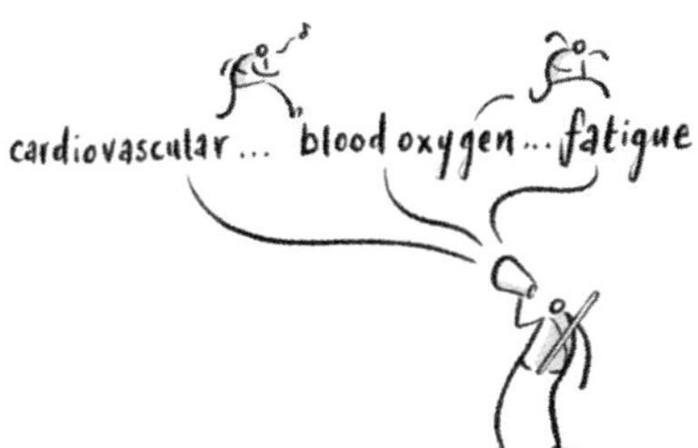

Teacher: Has anyone heard of the term 'cardiovascular endurance'?

[Several students put their hands up.]

Teacher: Has anyone heard parts of the phrase before, perhaps at the start or end of another word or phrase?

[Teacher pauses for a few seconds allowing students some time to think, then selects a student at random.]

Teacher: Harriet?

Harriet: I have heard of endurance before. I think it means something about lasting a long time.

Teacher: Brilliant, Harriet. Can you give me an example?

Harriet: The Tour de France is an endurance event.

Teacher: Really good example. What might good endurance look like in our current activity of rugby?

[Teacher pauses for a few seconds, allowing students some time to think, then asks them to tell their partner their thoughts.]

Teacher: What did you and your partner discuss *[pause]*, Dylan?

Dylan: We said that it means you don't get tired near the end of the game.

Teacher: Thanks, Dylan. What might that look like then? *[pause]* Ryan?

Ryan: Well it might mean that you don't make mistakes, like knock-ons or missed tackles, in the last 10 minutes of the game.

Teacher: Excellent, Ryan. And what is it called when you get tired near the end of the game and start making mistakes?

Ryan: Fatigue.

Teacher: Great. What do the muscles need to stop them becoming fatigued?

[Teacher pauses and allows students some thinking time. The teacher then asks the students to tell their partner.]

Teacher: What did you and your partner discuss *[pause]*, Arfa?

Arfa: Oxygen.

Teacher: Correct. Good knowledge, Lizzie. So, if we know that endurance means you can perform well for a long time and avoid fatigue, what do we understand by the term 'cardiovascular'? Have we seen any parts of the word in any other context?

[Teacher pauses for a few seconds, allowing students some time to think.]

Teacher: Tom, what do you think?

Tom: I don't know, Sir.

Teacher: Have you ever seen *Casualty, Holby City, House* or any programmes about A&E? *[Tom nods.]* What phrase do they use in those programmes when someone's heart stops beating?

Tom: They call it cardiac arrest.

Teacher: So, what do we think 'cardio' might refer to?

Tom: The heart?

Teacher: Good, Tom. Yes, the term 'cardiac' or 'cardio' refers to the heart. So now we know 'cardio' means 'heart' and 'endurance' means 'long lasting avoiding fatigue'. We also know that the muscles need oxygen to avoid fatigue. What organ do we use to get oxygen from the atmosphere into the blood?

[Teacher pauses for a few seconds allowing students some time to think.]

Teacher: Kim?

Kim: Lungs. Does that mean 'vascular' means 'lungs'? I thought the lungs were 'respiratory'?

Teacher: Correct, Kim. It is the lungs and they are in the respiratory system, but 'vascular' doesn't mean 'lungs'.

What is the system that connects the lungs and the heart and then takes the oxygen to the muscles?

Kim: The blood. So 'vascular' refers to blood?

Teacher: Nearly. It means 'a vessel that carries blood', such as?

Kim: Arteries and veins?

Teacher: Yes, well done. We will come on to blood vessels in more depth next year, but, for today, if we understand that the term 'cardio' refers to the heart, 'endurance' refers to long lasting and avoiding fatigue and 'vascular' refers to the blood vessels transporting oxygen from the lungs to the muscles, what does 'cardiovascular endurance' actually mean?

[Teacher pauses for a few seconds, allowing students some think time.]

Teacher: John?

John: How long your heart can pump blood to your muscles before they fatigue.

Teacher: What do the muscles need from the blood?

John: Oxygen.

Teacher: Why?

John: To keep working and not get tired or fatigued.

Teacher: How do we get oxygen into the bloodstream?

John: Through the lungs.

Teacher: Really good understanding, John. The correct definition is how well (efficiently) the heart (cardio), lungs and blood vessels (vascular) supply oxygen to the working muscles to avoid fatigue. That is, the efficiency of the heart and lungs to supply oxygen to the working muscles, avoiding fatigue. Repeat that back to me.

Class *[supported by the teacher prompts]*: The efficiency of the heart and lungs to supply oxygen to the working muscles, avoiding fatigue.

Teacher: 'Cardio' means?

Class: 'Heart'.

Teacher: Good. Now, what sports require us to have high levels of cardiovascular endurance and what will happen if you don't have good cardiovascular endurance?

[Teacher pauses and allows students some thinking time. The teacher then asks the students to tell their partner.]

Teacher: What did you and your partner discuss *[pause]*, Annie?

Annie: Football, and you might make mistakes and lose focus.

Teacher: So performance suffers, correct. Alex?

Alex: Marathon, and you will have to slow down and not run as fast.

Teacher: What will happen to your chances of winning the race?

Alex: Less chance and you might get injured if you push too hard.

Teacher: Well done. And one more *[pause]*, Louise?

Louise: Rugby. You might miss tackles but could also make mistakes if you are suffering from fatigue.

Teacher: Excellent knowledge. We will come back to this next lesson, but, for today, while you are warming up, I want you to think about how you can improve your cardiovascular endurance.

---

3. Success Narratives

From the very first lesson in September, we need to set the bar of expectation high, as this will enable us to really challenge our students. This is far easier to do in the theory element of GCSE PE. Keep the very best Year 11 books from your most successful students and show them to students as they start out on their GCSE PE venture. Use these books to point out the features of successful work, referring back to them throughout the course. This might include:

♦ Neatly presented work.

♦ Well-organised work, homing in on key information, with titles underlined.

♦ Detailed explanations and answers to questions.

♦ Evidence of metacognition (e.g. planning of tasks; monitoring linked to task, self and use of strategy; evaluating the effectiveness of applied strategies).

♦ High-quality homework.

This can also be done practically. Yes, it is trickier, but it can be achieved nonetheless, perhaps through outlining basic expectations surrounding effort, kit, punctuality, changing time, standards, health and safety regarding hair, jewellery, etc. Time spent early in September establishing these expectations and how to be successful in the subject, with regular reminders throughout the year, can ensure standards are maintained. The high expectations around procedural and presentational elements then afford you more time to refine skills and you waste less time ensuring that everyone is ready to learn. With regards to the quality of performance, at the beginning of each unit it is worth showing a short video of a top-level athlete performing the full-context element of that activity. Whether you are showing a video of an elite athlete or a student, or asking a student for a live demonstration, the key feature needs to be the reference you make to how and why it is a successful performance and how the other students can replicate that in their own performances. The subtlety is in linking the progress and success to replicable behaviours. Highlight the fact that the final successful skill is the icing on the cake, but the cake is baked over a long time through those replicable behaviours that you are looking for. Using student success stories may also lead to their peers developing their self-efficacy through a vicarious experience.[4] By this, we mean that when students see someone who they subconsciously perceive as an equal completing the skill, it will support their willingness to try and feel that they can be successful in the skill or task.

4. Formative Assessment

Dylan Wiliam suggests that the regular use of minute-by-minute and day-by-day classroom formative assessment can substantially improve student achievement.[5] In PE, the best teachers take information from the students, use it and then intervene to ensure that students can make the improvements that Dylan is referring to. The various components are identified in the diagram on pages 26–27.

---

4   Albert Bandura, Self-Efficacy: Toward a Unifying Theory of Behaviour Change, *Psychological Review*, 84(2) (1977): 191–215. Available at: https://educational-innovation.sydney.edu.au/news/pdfs/Bandura%201977.pdf.

5   Dylan Wiliam, *Embedded Formative Assessment* (Bloomington, IN: Solution Tree Press, 2011).

Formative Assessment

Getting the best possible evidence about what students (responses from all) have learnt and then using this information to inform teaching and curriculum.

Quizzes and multiple-choice questions

Include common misconceptions within the possible answers, have two or three distractors, have more than one correct answer and use a variety of stems. Incorrect answers should be plausible.

Students should be able to explain why the answer is correct and why the others are not.

Use regular quizzing to reveal to students where the gaps in their knowledge are.

Use checklists alongside quizzes to support and allow students to assess their own strengths and areas of weakness.

Reading work or observing students *at work*

Monitor body language and classroom atmosphere to gain a sense of how students are coping.

Be clear on what you are looking for – what is the focus?

Use a formative assessment book to check students work (engage students in the discussion).

There is no point finding something that needs fixing and not fixing it.

Look for good student examples and use these as worked examples.

Atomising
(assessing composite parts of a complex task)

Explicitly teach all of the steps including the most basic starting point.

Break down all parts and give feedback on all aspects.

Plan all of the steps beforehand.

Elicit understanding of why students use certain structures and processes.

Don't move on until each step is mastered. This should include planning, monitoring and evaluating.

Explicitly teach metacognitive thinking around the most difficult processes or concepts.

Diagnostic questions

Based on feedback from formative assessment, plan questions and who you are going to ask, including the whole class.

Closed questions are fine, if used appropriately.

Factual knowledge is as important as procedural analysis and evaluation.

Use elaborative, probing and Socratic questions to check for deeper understanding and whether students know why the answer is correct.

Don't accept 'I don't know' responses.

This inherently links to the principle of challenge. If we are able to take information from students' outputs and use it to shape what we, as teachers, do next, it will ensure that the level of challenge can be both individualised and targeted, keeping students in the struggle zone. The outline below shows how this may be done using diagnostic questions practically when teaching tackling in rugby:

Last time I saw this group, Oscar struggled with the ring of steel (arms wrapped around the waist of the opposing player). He kept letting go and needed to unpick why. The class weren't clear on why the leg drive was necessary in completing the tackle. Ronnie kept forgetting to roll away after completing the tackle. Brad was unsure where he needed to put his head during the side-on tackle.

This preparation from the previous lesson is used to shape the questions when recapping the tackle. The teacher plans the questions and who they are going to ask. In the lesson, it might look something like this:

Teacher: Last lesson we looked at tackling. Why is tackling a fundamental skill in rugby? [*Pause for a few seconds*] Think about your answer for 10 seconds before I come to one of you … Matthew, let's start with you.

Matthew: I don't know, Sir.

Teacher: Ok, no problem, Matthew. What would happen if John had the ball and nobody could tackle him?

Matthew: He would score a try.

Teacher: Brilliant, yes, he would score. So why is tackling really important then?

Matthew: To stop the other team scoring a try.

Teacher: And what would happen after the tackling? Could we compete for the ball?

Matthew: Yes, the tackle could lead to a ruck.

Teacher: Brilliant, and what's a ruck then … think for 10 seconds … now discuss the answer with the person sat next to you for 5 seconds [*the teacher would ensure that everyone has a talk partner*]. 3, everyone looking at me; 2, finishing your conversations, thank you, Steve; and 1, … Phillip, what do you think?

Phillip: We think a ruck is where at least one player from each team competes for contact over the ball.

Teacher: Good start, Phillip. Hopefully we will move on to rucking, but let's just check that everyone is happy with tackling. Oh, actually, what would happen if the tackler didn't let go of the opposing player after a tackle … Ronnie?

Ronnie: It would be a penalty to the other team.

Teacher: Excellent, Ronnie. Why would it be a penalty, do you think?

Ronnie: The tackler must release the player they have tackled or make an attempt to roll away.

Teacher: Good, Ronnie. So we must make sure that we let go and roll away when the referee confirms the tackle has been made. OK, so what else can we remember about tackling then? [*Pause for a few seconds*] … Oscar?

Oscar: Cheek-to-cheek, Sir, where your head is behind the tackler's leg if it's from the side.

Teacher: Good. And why is that important, do we think … Brad?

Brad: So you can tackle them easier.

Teacher: Yes, it will help with that, but think, Brad; if Oscar is running towards you with the ball, what will his knees be doing?

Brad: Driving up so he can try and get through the tackle.

Teacher: Yes, and if your head is in front of the leg and not behind, what might happen?

Brad: Oh, I see, I will get kneed in the head.

Teacher: Yes, well done. So your head always goes behind to protect yourself but also to increase your chance of tackling successfully. So, what do we do with our arms then … Oscar?

Oscar: Hold on to them.

Teacher: Yes, but where on the body and why is it important that we hold on to the other player?

Oscar: Their waist, and we should hold on so they can't run away.

Teacher: Yes, well done. What would happen if we didn't have the ring of steel [teacher shows the action]? What could the attacker do, if you tackled him to the ground but did not have the ring of steel?

Oscar: He could get up and keep on running and maybe score a try.

Teacher: Exactly, so do you see why the ring of steel is so important now, Oscar? OK, to build on this, what would happen if I had my head in the correct position, ensured I had the ring of steel but didn't use my legs to drive into the contact? 10 seconds to think on your own … 5 seconds to talk to your partner … Greg, what did you and Tom discuss?

Greg: We said that we would just be holding them, and they could keep walking or offload the ball.

Teacher: OK, what could you do to prevent this then … Patrick?

Patrick: Drive into them with your shoulder, but use your legs to ensure you have enough power to take them to the ground.

Teacher: Excellent, so that is what we are going to practise quickly now before we move on to rucking.

Ryan De Gruchy, deputy leader of PE at Durrington High School, explains how he recently used a formative assessment strategy to promote healthy challenge in his Year 9 badminton unit:

As I was teaching the flick serve, I started with place markers in the two front corners of the service box. The success was varied as I walked around the group and observed students at work. I noticed four students were successful with landing the shuttle on the markers consistently. I could then check their understanding of when and why to use this type of serve. I was happy that they understood this, so I moved them on to looking at the flick serve to the back of the court and asked them to think deeply about why this was a useful variation to have. After a few more minutes of practising, I was able to move them on to a game where, if they won the point within two shots of the serve, they got an extra point, highlighting the importance of the serve, but also the use of variations to outwit their opponents.

Ryan used the formative assessment strategies of observing students at work and diagnostic questioning. Through these strategies he was able to move a few students on to a slightly more difficult task, thus ensuring they were in the struggle zone. Had he moved the whole class on, then some students would have been in the panic zone, which may have affected their progress negatively. This was achievable due to his use of formative assessment as a tool to promote challenge.

5. Think Now and Think Hard About It

The anchor effect suggests that our perceptions are influenced by the first piece of information we receive on a topic.[1] For example, if you see a car advertised for £10,000 and you get it for £9,000, you will think you got a good deal because you paid less than the asking price. In reality, it may have only been worth £8,000, but you had anchored your expectations at £10,000 as that was the first piece of information you received. As PE teachers, we need to ensure that students' first exposure to any new activity is to something challenging that makes them think. This will create the perception that success in this activity will require thinking. 'Think now' tasks – placed at the start of the lesson, while setting up, or prior to the warm-up – can help to achieve this and are designed to stimulate deep thought. Examples could include:

- A difficult question that will stimulate thinking. (These can be useful to create connections across topics or ideas.)

- A challenging game-play scenario. For example, in a football match, you are 1–0 down with two minutes left and you have a wide free kick 40 yards out. What would you do?

- A picture of a sports performer and a question: what is the most important component of fitness for this athlete and why?

---

1   Daniel Kahneman, *Thinking, Fast and Slow* (London: Allen Lane, 2011), loc. 1998–2180.

Reflective Questions

♦ How do you ensure that your subject knowledge, across all the sporting disciplines and activities that you teach, is strong enough to stretch and challenge all students?

♦ How do you ensure that you know your students' strengths and weaknesses so that you are able to keep them all in the struggle zone?

♦ Are you confident in your ability to answer the hardest questions that your students will be asked? Are you able to model your thinking?

♦ Do you insist on the use of PE-specific vocabulary and terminology at all times in both Key Stage 3 and 4?

♦ Do you use a variety of formative assessment strategies to ensure that your teaching challenges students as individual learners?

♦ How do you get students thinking from the start of every lesson?

♦ How do you get students to think deeply and make links across topics or activities?

♦ How do you encourage a culture of struggle and challenge with all of your teaching groups?

Chapter 2

Explanation

Explanation and clarity of instruction – whether outlining how to bat in Year 8 rounders or explaining how to set up a task to 32 Year 7 students in gymnastics – are fundamental for PE teachers for a number of reasons. It is as important lower down the school as it is in the exam years at Key Stage 4. We need to understand a large body of content and sporting principles and we have to transfer that understanding to our students, for them to be able to decipher, use and apply it to a range of complex contexts. Many of these ideas are abstract and come with individual complexities linked to prior background knowledge. Furthermore, the students will have a wide range of misconceptions that need to be unpicked before we can begin to successfully build and develop new knowledge and skills.

As PE teachers, there are four questions that we should consider when thinking about explanation:

1 How do we tether new knowledge to what students already know and can do? Psychologists refer to the framework of things we know – our infinite storehouse of knowledge – and how we organise that information as a schema. Following the evidence review conducted by the Education Endowment Foundation (EEF), it is widely accepted that the human brain is more likely to absorb knowledge if it links to existing schemata.[1] For

---

1 Thomas Perry, Rosanna Lea, Clara Rübner Jørgensen, Philippa Cordingley, Kimron Shapiro and Deborah Youdell, *Cognitive Science Approaches in the Classroom: A Review of the Evidence* (London: Education Endowment Foundation, 2021). Available at: https://d2tic4wvo1iusb.cloudfront.net/production/documents/guidance/Cognitive_science_approaches_in_the_classroom_-_A_review_of_the_evidence.pdf?v=1708411030; Thomas Perry, Rosanna Lea, Clara Rübner Jørgensen, Philippa Cordingley, Kimron Shapiro and Deborah Youdell, *Cognitive Science in the Classroom: Evidence and Practice Review* (London: Education Endowment Foundation, 2021). Available at: https://d2tic4wvo1iusb.cloudfront.net/production/documents/guidance/Cognitive_Science_in_the_classroom_-_Evidence_and_practice_review.pdf?v=1706001108.

example, if students already have a sound understanding of power and how it is needed in sprinting, they are more likely to be able to explain why plyometrics could be used to enhance performance.

2   How can we introduce new ideas in clear steps? It is worth noting that we need to be able to formatively assess each of these steps, providing feedback along the way where required. We know from cognitive science that the working memory (the part of the brain that holds, processes and manipulates information) has a limit to what it can do – known as cognitive load.[2] If we try to present students with too much information at once, there is a real risk that we will overload their working memory, resulting in confusion and a lack of processing capacity. Therefore, I'd suggest that we should only give students up to three things to think about, use and understand at any one time for all new skills we teach them. In the same way, we would teach tackling in rugby in small chunks, building up the complexity over time due to the safety element.

3   How do we avoid the curse of the expert? It's often hardest to teach the sport you are most confident in playing. The reason for this is, as experts who are teaching novices, we have to be very careful when explaining new ideas, strategies or concepts not to ignore knowledge that we take for granted. The risk is that we forget what we know. Our students will not have the same implicit knowledge. For example, when teaching spirometry, we are assuming that students understand that tidal volume includes both inhalation and exhalation. If they don't, they will struggle to fully understand the term 'tidal volume' let alone the rest of spirometry. As a practical example, when teaching dribbling in football, we are assuming that students can control the ball and

---

2   John Sweller, Cognitive Load Theory, Learning Difficulty, and Instructional Design, *Learning and Instruction*, 4(4) (1994): 295–312. Available at: https://www.sciencedirect.com/science/article/abs/pii/0959475294900035.

use all parts of their foot to manipulate it under close control with their head up. If they can't, they will struggle to perform the skill in isolation let alone in a game situation with the added pressure of decision making, teammates and opposing players.

4   How do we make abstract ideas concrete? This is linked to the curse of the expert. We should think carefully about how we can make abstract ideas concrete and tangible to students – for example, lever systems and how we use the example of a wheelbarrow as a concrete example when introducing a second-class lever system.

Explanation Strategies

This section aims to outline how we may begin to answer these four questions in both theory and practical PE.

1. Stories

Stories are an integral part of human existence; knowledge is passed down through the generations via storytelling. This is the same vehicle used by our ancestors who passed their wisdom on for thousands of years. The best PE teachers will use stories to support their explanation. The good news is that we have a plethora of stories available to us. As PE teachers, we should make it our business to know the history of the sports or concepts we are teaching and use this to enhance our explanations. This can also be the case when trying to make abstract concepts more concrete in the students' minds. For example:

♦ High jump: tell the story of how it was traditionally the scissor technique that dominated. Athletes would land on their feet in sand. Then the development of the Western roll took place. Unpick how this came to the fore and why other competitors disregarded the technique, leading to the evolution of landing on a mat as opposed to in a sand pit. Dick Fosbury modernised the sport with his innovative approach and raised the bar, excuse the pun, for future competitors. He wanted to get his centre of gravity even closer to the bar while maintaining momentum from the run up, hence going backwards over the bar as opposed to the Western roll where you cross the bar facing the ground. At each stage, allow students the opportunity to experience the skill. Show the students how the technique has evolved and allow them the time to understand the flaws in the previous techniques, leading to the Fosbury flop emerging as the most effective high jump technique.

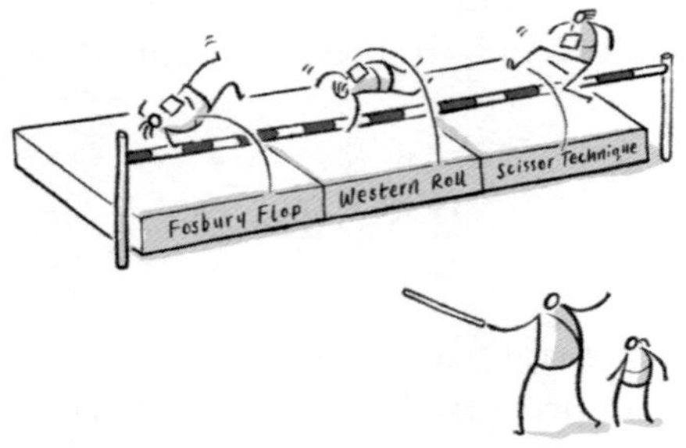

♦ Technology in sport: when discussing technological developments in sport, tell the story of Frank Lampard's disallowed goal in the 2010 World Cup and the introduction of goal line technology. Another example is talking the students through the evolution of skin-tight jerseys in rugby union. The 2003 World Cup winning rugby coach Clive Woodward showed clips of England winger Jason Robinson being overcome by last-ditch scrag tackles while wearing the old baggy cotton jersey to a group of world-class coaches. The coaches could not identify the common reason he was unable to score, until it was highlighted to them, thus leading to the introduction of the skin-tight jersey.

♦ Lever systems: stories can also be used to make abstract concepts concrete. When discussing levers, use the concrete example of a seesaw for a first-class lever and a wheelbarrow for a second-class lever. The mechanical advantage comes in when you start to think about whether you could increase the distance between the wheel and the handle, which allows for increased weight to be moved with less effort being applied. Obviously, we can't increase the length of our limbs (levers), but we could use a tennis racket, for example, to increase our power. Tether the new information to the idea of playing in the park or going to a farm (places where students would have their own childhood memories of playing on a seesaw or using a wheelbarrow).

Stories work because they are built upon students' prior knowledge, and this supports the complex ideas behind them by putting them into a real-world context that the students can understand. The human aspect of stories makes them highly memorable for the students.

2. Prior Knowledge and Existing Misconceptions

If we are trying to build upon what students already know or tether new information to existing schemata, then the most logical place to start is finding out what students already know and can do. Alongside this, though, it is just as important to find out what misconceptions students may have, as these will add to the complexity of progressing their understanding. The balance here is finding out helpful information about what students do and do not know and how we can build on that. This should then be used to inform your explanation. There are a number of ways we can do this:

♦ **Demonstration or visual prompt.** We could use an image when introducing a new topic, followed by a series of questions. For example, when introducing the cardiac cycle, show the students a diagram and then question them about it. (e.g. can you name each part of the cycle? What does each part do? What is the direction of the blood? What happens in the lungs? In the muscles? Why is it important? How does it link to respiration or gaseous exchange?). This is equally powerful in practical lessons: demonstrating a skill and then probing students' understanding of the sport and the procedural knowledge required to improve the skill. For example, when introducing a lay-up in basketball, show students the skill several times, then probe them about how to carry it out, when to use it and why it's important. (e.g. what are the three key teaching points of the lay-up? Where do you aim on the backboard? What is the footwork pattern? Why do you need to jump with the ball? When would you use a lay-up? Why is it an effective shot to use? How would you perform the skill differently from the other side or if a defender was putting you under pressure?). These types of prompts will provide you with a wealth of information about what the students know; the next step will be to see what they can do.

♦ **Tell me or show me what you know about.** Very simply, name the topic or concept and ask the students to either tell you what they know or show you what they can do (e.g. what do you know about hooliganism? Write down five things. What are the three different types of pass in netball? In pairs, show me).

♦ **Pre-empt the misconceptions.** As we are the experts in our field, rather than waiting for common misconceptions to arise, let's unpick them early on. For example, when playing badminton, students will often stand square on. In theory, they often think that you should have more protein in your diet than fats. These are both relatively standard misconceptions, so why not present them to students at the start of the unit and discuss why they are incorrect. This way you are not relying on them to reveal their misconceptions but making them explicit from the start, allowing you more time to focus on deepening their knowledge base.

3. Open the Curiosity Gap

Curiosity directly generates what we want as PE teachers: students thinking deeply about a concept, skill or topic in our subject. We can use this to our advantage. Show students something intriguing that will make them think deeply, ask questions and be keen to find out more. Examples could include: details of the daily diet of Michael Phelps in training, a short clip of Lance Armstrong talking about blood doping, an article by Simone Biles on the impact of sport on her mental health, or a video of a 30-shot rally at Wimbledon.

Following this, explain to the students that by the end of the lesson they will be able to explain what they have seen. This will spark their natural inquisition and should make them want to delve deeper into the curiosity gap that you have ignited.

4. Explain and Probe

New ideas, concepts or topics need to be explained. We do need to explicitly tell students about them in order to share our knowledge. This is perfectly acceptable; we shouldn't be ashamed of 'teacher talk'. After all, we know stuff and students don't, so we have to tell them.

The best PE teachers are extremely skilled at twinning this with expert questioning and modelling. Specific modelling and questioning strategies are discussed in Chapters 3 and 5, but it is paramount to also mention their role in explanation. For example, when explaining the principle of attack in football, we can use a range of questions to shape and develop students' understanding of our explanation (e.g.

what are the key principles of attack in football? How do we use height and width to create goal scoring opportunities? Why do we need to ensure we have depth? How can we create more shooting opportunities? What is the risk vs reward balance, and why is it important in the game?). At the same time, you can use demonstrations or worked examples to support students' understanding – from simply setting up a phase of play to show the space available to showing them an intricate pattern leading to a shot on target.

In order to shape your explanations and support students' understanding, the principle is clear: all explanations should be coupled with asking questions about, and effective modelling of, the idea under discussion.

5. Building Explanations

John Hattie proposes that there is a difference between surface and deep learning. In simple terms, surface learning is knowing key information about a topic,[3] deep learning refers to how we can use, link, extend and apply this knowledge. This has important implications for PE teachers when planning our explanations and how quickly to move on to the next one. We need to make sure that students are secure in their surface learning before moving on to deep learning.

Consider the process of understanding the full context of a hockey game. To grasp this, the students will need to be secure with the following knowledge and skills:

♦ Grip of the stick.

♦ Rules of the game.

♦ How to pass and dribble the ball.

♦ How to shoot and the principles of attack.

---

3   John Hattie, The Science of Learning. Keynote speech presented at Osiris World-Class Schools Convention, London (2014).

♦ Legalities of tackling and principles of defence.

♦ Understanding of positions.

If any of these essential pieces of the puzzle are missing, the students will struggle to fully apply their knowledge and understand the game. Hence the need to consider during our lesson planning what knowledge and skills the students will need – and how our explanation will support this – in order to fully understand the more demanding work. This is equally important for curriculum leaders when planning medium- and long-term schemes of work.

6. Be an Expert in All Aspects of PE

According to the Sutton Trust report, *What Makes Great Teaching?*, subject knowledge is ranked as the top contributor.[4] This can prove problematic for PE teachers as most of us have to teach a large number of sports or activities; some of these will fall outside of our specialism or, at the very best, we won't be as confident with their delivery. A gymnast will undoubtedly feel very confident teaching gymnastics to a top-level gymnast. They will feel more than able to extend their understanding, identify and address misconceptions, respond to their questions and add depth and breadth to their explanations, while being able to model high-quality skills. They are less likely to feel this way about all of the other sports or activities they may have to teach.

However, we need to make it our priority to develop our subject knowledge across everything that we teach. This will support our explanation but also the quality of our formative assessment, questioning, modelling and feedback. This can be done in the following ways:

♦ Step out of your comfort zone. Play the sport, see what mistakes you make, develop your confidence with the

---

4 Coe et al., *What Makes Great Teaching?*

nuances of the skills, model them, and get feedback from your colleagues. Repeat this process until you know exactly what to do, how to do it, what it should look like, what the common misconceptions are and how you explain them in the best possible way. This can be with colleagues in your school or further afield, such as a national governing body or a local sports club.

♦ Observe colleagues. Watch the experts teach the areas where you feel less confident. Learn from their expertise and invite them to observe you and learn from yours. Sharing your strengths can only lead to a better learning experience for the students.

♦ Know the specification, curriculum and assessment criteria inside out. Make it your business to fully scrutinise every aspect of what you are expected to teach.

♦ Use exam resources. Sit and mark exam papers. Use online standardisation and moderators' reports. Identify your own knowledge gaps and plan how you are going to fill them.

♦ Practise your explanations, including practical demonstrations, with an expert and ask them for feedback. Use this expert to watch your lessons and support you to refine the clarity and effectiveness of your explanations and progressions.

The level of challenge in your lessons starts with the quality of your explanations, and these stand or fall on your level of subject knowledge – make it your priority to make them consistently brilliant.

7. Lift the Veil

Another potential problem with the curse of the expert is expecting students to understand the value in what we ask them to do. We know that if we develop students' understanding of how to dig and set with the correct technique in volleyball, including developing their decision making, that it will support the quality of their game play over time. We often forget to share that wisdom, to explain why we aren't just going straight into full games. It seems relatively simple and straightforward, but too often we, as PE teachers, forget to explain the purpose of the task we are asking students to complete. Short-, medium- and long-term plans for where we intend our students to go should be explicitly shared. Explaining to students the rationale behind the tasks they are doing, linking to the bigger picture of their physical development, is a good starting point for this.

PE teachers often start with the 'So, today we are going to …' before explaining the why. A fundamental component of explanation is to lift the veil on why we are asking students to do something and what we are thinking. The EEF Teaching and Learning Toolkit suggests, through a meta-analysis of studies, that getting students to think more explicitly about their learning has a positive impact on their attainment.[5] Metacognition is the way in which learners purposefully monitor and direct their own learning. In simple terms, metacognition is about students understanding and improving their own planning, monitoring and evaluating of their learning, and developing the tools they need to do this through knowledge of the task, self and strategy. We will return to this in Chapters 3, 5 and 6.

Lifting the veil is about making students acutely aware of all of the implicit processes we go through as the expert in the room. It is also about including them in the learning journey; we want to explicitly tell them about the thinking behind it, rather than expecting them to blindly follow our instructions. We wouldn't go for a run without knowing where we are going, so we shouldn't expect our students to do the same thing in our lessons. We need to give students an insight into why they are doing what they are doing at any given moment in a lesson or series of lessons. Ultimately, metacognition is about changing students' behaviour, so the gold standard is for your students to create those links and be able to explain their thought processes, linked to planning, monitoring and evaluating their own learning. This is a huge cultural shift and needs to be built over time, but it will lead to students who are better able to self-regulate, more often and more effectively, and hopefully fewer complaints of 'Why can't we just play a full game?'

Reflective Questions

- How do you find your students' prior knowledge and starting points in a new activity?

- Are you explicitly planning to use stories as part of your explanation process?

---

5   See: https://educationendowmentfoundation.org.uk/education-evidence/ teaching-learning-toolkit.

- How do you tether new knowledge to pre-existing knowledge?

- Do you explicitly involve students in your thought processes when explaining the purpose of tasks?

- How do you break up your explanations with modelling and questioning?

- How do you develop your subject knowledge to support your explanations?

Chapter 3

Modelling

Modelling is the bread and butter of high-quality PE teaching. In our subject, the students may have never seen the sporting activity we are teaching, let alone understand the complexities of the skills we are asking them to perform. Our ability to model correctly will directly impact the students' ability to really understand how to perform a skill and why that skill is fundamental to the success of that activity. We teach a huge array of practical activities at Key Stage 3 and 4, all with an eclectic range of skills that underpin success in that sport. Just as we wouldn't explain how to use a map in a geography lesson without physically showing the students one, we wouldn't explain how to complete a task or perform a skill in PE without showing the students what it looks like.

Barak Rosenshine suggests that effective modelling can support student confidence and student performance. When taking students through a difficult task, modelling a procedure in small step-by-step chunks, followed by focused practice and repeating the cycle, is highly effective.[1] This is a prudent message, linked to cognitive load theory, as it is important that our modelling takes the limitations of working memory into account.

Another challenge for PE teachers to grapple with when thinking about modelling is that we will be required to model many different things – for example:

♦ How to perform a specific skill within a physical activity or sport in ever-changing situations.

---

1 Barak Rosenshine, Principles of Instruction: Research-Based Strategies That All Teachers Should Know, *American Educator*, 38(1) (2012): 12–19, 39. Available at: https://www.aft.org/sites/default/files/periodicals/Rosenshine.pdf.

49

- How to perform a complete example of a physical activity or game – for example, a full game of basketball or a floor routine in gymnastics.

- How to analyse and interpret data (in a GCSE exam paper context).

- How to answer 6- and 9-mark exam questions and apply knowledge to unfamiliar situations (again, in a GCSE exam paper context).

- How to develop the core values of sport, such as determination, resilience, excellence and sportsmanship.

I think there's a key point to be made here about the importance of modelling in sport. Success or failure is based on fine margins (e.g. a slight change to body position can make a significant difference to a badminton smash). With this in mind, it is really important to model the precise way to carry out that particular action, to avoid embedding bad habits. It is worth thinking about some of the issues inherent in each of these modelled areas in turn before we think about strategies that can be used to address them.

How to Perform a Specific Skill Within a Physical Activity or Sport in Ever-Changing Situations

When it comes to secondary PE, students might be performing skills that they have never attempted before. Therefore we will need to precisely model all of the steps involved in the successful execution of the skill in isolation, under increasing pressure and in full-context situations. Don't make any assumptions about students' knowledge of any of the steps and implicit processes we go through in the successful completion of the skill. Not only will this support students in understanding the best way to perform the skill, but in informing their decisions about when to use the skill within the physical activity.

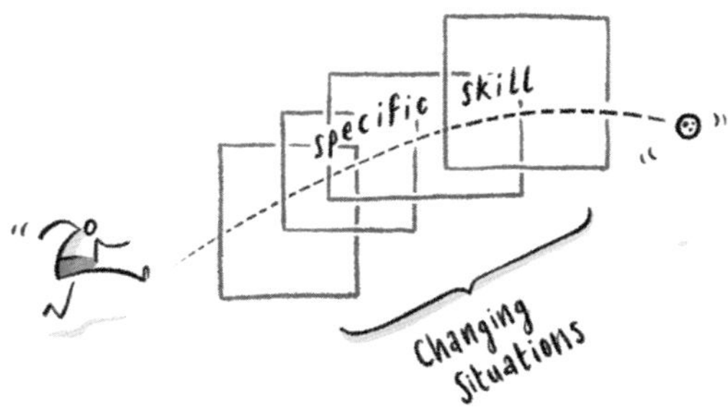

One question that tends to arise when we think about modelling is: 'When should the teacher model themselves, and when should they use a student or a video?' The answer should always address who is going to get the message across to the group of learners most effectively. This is obviously going to be dependent on the school, the class, the teacher, the skill, the students and the timing within the lesson and scheme of work. The first time you introduce a new skill, I would advocate for teacher modelling. The reason for this is that the teacher can exaggerate certain movements to draw students' attention and support their understanding, slow the skill down to highlight certain aspects, and pause and question, all while being able to explain the key elements to focus on within the skill.

From my experience, most teachers will model skills themselves as much as possible. If for some reason they cannot model, then a student or a video is perfectly acceptable. If students are struggling with specific elements and, following the teacher's model, they still can't perform the skill, then a carefully selected student model is useful as it creates a vicarious experience which will support their self-efficacy.[2] The student being used to model must be one that the majority of the class can relate to in terms of ability. For example, not

---

2   Bandura, *Self-Efficacy*.

using your Team GB hockey player to model the slap shot, instead using someone who can do it well but is relatively inexperienced in the sport and not seen as a 'strong' performer by the other students. The thought pattern goes along the lines of: 'You, as the teacher, should be able to perform the skill, but if a student in the group can do it, then I, as a fellow student, should be able to do it too.' Video analysis is also useful, usually when looking at an individual or a small group. Specifically, if there is a very small element that they can't seem to get right, then showing the students the skill in slow motion will be hugely beneficial. How to do this is discussed later on in this chapter. In my experience, this works best for more closed skills with multifaceted techniques, such as throwing in athletics field events.

The added layer of complexity comes from the depth of subject knowledge and the magnitude of skills that we need to model. Linked in with this is the ability to explain, question, allow sufficient practice and give purposeful feedback. If you take a typical Key Stage 3 long-term plan and work out the sheer number of elements that require modelling, and all the variations that come with this, it is vast. In order to model all aspects of the subject effectively, a strong subject knowledge base is crucial. An example plan might look like this:

Date	Activity	Skills
	Football	Passing and receiving, shooting, dribbling, tackling, heading.
	Rugby union	Passing and receiving, tackling, rucking, mauling, kicking, scrummaging, evasion.

Date	Activity	Skills
	Handball	Passing and receiving, shooting, dribbling, blocking, defending.
	Netball	Passing and receiving, shooting, defending, footwork, movement.
	Hockey	Passing and receiving, shooting, tackling, dribbling.
	Badminton	Service, clears, drops, smash.
	Basketball	Passing and receiving, shooting, dribbling, blocking, defending.
	Table tennis	Service, push shots, drives, topspin, backspin, sidespin, lobs.
	Gymnastics	Rolls, balances, rotations, transitions.
	Dance	Jumps, turns, action, space, dynamics, relationships.
	Athletics (field)	Grip, release, take off, approach, flight, landing.
	Softball	Bowling, batting, fielding, throwing, catching.

Date	Activity	Skills
	Tennis	Service, forehand, backhand, lob, smash, volley.
	Athletics (track)	Start phase, acceleration phase, drive phase, deceleration phase, bend running, changeover.
	Rounders	Bowling, batting, fielding, throwing, catching.
	Cricket	Bowling, batting, fielding, throwing, catching.

This proves challenging for a teacher, let alone a student. Therefore, a further consideration when modelling in practical lessons is the idea of working memory: the brain's capacity to hold, manipulate and process information. It is generally agreed that the brain has the capacity to hold and process between five and nine elements at any one time.[3] For some of our students with a lower starting point, this may be as low as two or three. The limit of working memory has implications when modelling and giving instructions in a practical setting, as most students will struggle with being given too many steps at once. For example, when teaching serving in table tennis, we need to break the skill down into its composite parts: open palm for holding the ball, the ball must be above table height prior to the release, the ball must be thrown up off the palm of your hand by at least 6 inches, you must hit the ball behind the line of the table, the ball must bounce on your side of the table and then your

---

3   George A. Miller, The Magical Number Seven, Plus or Minus Two: Some Limits on Our Capacity for Processing Information, *Psychological Review*, 63(2) (1956): 81–97.

opponent's side, the ball can be hit forehand or backhand and can be brushed from low to high to generate topspin or cut under to generate backspin. We would then model up to five of these composite parts at any one time. If we were to introduce the entire procedure and all of the elements at once, we would potentially cognitively overload our students, flooding their working memory with too much information.

Let's consider another example from a team sport. When teaching passing in netball, we need to break the skill down into: receiving the ball (statically and dynamically), following the footwork rule, understanding the different types of pass and when to use them, passing when the receiver is stood still vs when they are moving into space. Again, we would need to model how to receive the ball, explaining how and why this is important. Once this is secure, we would then move on to explain the footwork rule, then receiving the ball while on the move. At each stage, the students would need explicit modelling, punctuated with questioning and feedback. Once students have had enough time to practise each specific element of receiving the ball, we would then begin to deconstruct passing. We would have to model the pass as a static activity without any pressure, building up the pressure until we reach real game play. This would need to be modelled at each stage of progression, and we need to follow the process for all three types of pass.

How to Perform a Complete Example of a Physical Activity or Game

Students have to learn how to apply their knowledge of skill execution in a number of different sporting activities. Each sport or physical activity has different ways to use the core skills successfully to outwit your opponent or maximise your performance. For example, to defend in rugby, the core skill of tackling could be used in a drift defence, an umbrella defence or a blitz defence. The skill also has variations, such as front, rear, side, smother and chop tackle. So, simply put, there are five different tackles and three defensive strategies that students need to understand and be able to use to be successful in rugby. Each of these will need to be explicitly taught. As with tier 2 words in Chapter 1, students may already be familiar with a number of different skills in a completely different context. This may lead to misconceptions which will need to be addressed, potentially through modelling. For example, in football, students would use the skill of passing, which is the movement of the ball between teammates, to play a diagonal ball between two defenders for an onrushing attacker. This is very different in hockey. Students may have the misconception that a diagonal pass will be appropriate when presented with two flat defenders in a two-vs-two formation as this was successful in football. However, in hockey, the best way to break down two flat defenders would be with a square pass followed by a straight pass to a diagonal running teammate. This would need to be explicitly modelled to students along with explaining the underpinning reasons why.

How to Analyse and Interpret Data

Analysing and interpreting data is an essential aspect of many career paths in sport: sports scientists, physiotherapists, performance analysts, coaches and nutritionists to name but a few. Hence, the introduction of the AQA GCSE PE unit 3.1.4: Use of data. This involves recording data in tables, analysing it, displaying it graphically, looking for trends and patterns, spotting anomalous results, describing and explaining these trends and then drawing conclusions. Each step is fraught with complexities for the average teenager. Graph drawing, for instance, can provide plenty of opportunities for error if not modelled correctly (e.g.

getting the axes right, using the correct scales, including the units, plotting the points accurately, drawing the line or bar). An important issue for us as PE teachers is not making assumptions; students will need to use data throughout the maths curriculum, so find out how your maths department teaches these topics. What are the common misconceptions? Factor these into your explicit modelling of each step.

How to Answer 6- and 9-Mark Exam Questions and Apply Knowledge to Unfamiliar Situations

Students really struggle with applying their knowledge to a range of sports or scenarios. While they might have an excellent understanding of the definitions of the components of fitness and types of training, if they are presented with an exam question that asks them to evaluate the appropriateness of plyometric and fartlek training for a 100m sprinter, they will often struggle to use this knowledge to answer the question. With this in mind, we need to model our own thinking process when we are tackling this kind of question. If we make all of the implicit processes we go through explicit to students, supporting them with their planning of how to tackle this type of question, it will, over time, support them to apply their knowledge in higher-mark exam questions.

How to Develop the Core Values of Sport

PE has many unique elements when it comes to the secondary curriculum, one of which is the balance between being a successful sports performer – whether that is as a county-level trampolinist, a regional rugby player or a team England dancer – and being a well-rounded individual who has developed a set of wider societal values through sport. All schools have individual mottos or slogans. These tend to be themed around students learning how to be the best version of themselves as people. At Durrington High School our motto is 'Going beyond your best, through kindness, aspiration, perseverance and pride'. As PE teachers, it is paramount that we uphold these values, but – more importantly – we must embody and model them in all aspects of our school life, including during extracurricular clubs or fixtures.

Let's now consider some of the most effective modelling strategies that we can use.

Modelling Strategies

1. Live Modelling, the Metacognitive Way

When we want to model any kind of task, skill or activity to our students – whether it is an answer to a 9-mark exam question, how to perform a handspring in gymnastics, address a misconception in bowling in cricket or a short-passing activity in football – the best thing we can do is show them how to do it ourselves, with a direct explanation of the thought processes that underpin it. All too often, we show an aspirational model answer in PE theory or simply tell the students what they need to do in the practical without showing them how to produce that answer or correct their technique. We need to model, model and model some more. We too often make the assumption that students understand and have the bandwidth to apply our comments to their own practice in practical tasks. This is the same in theory; we need to show them how to answer the questions, not merely provide model answers. It is the explicit modelling of the processes we go through coupled with why and how that will support students in our subject.

Live modelling is underpinned by a relatively straightforward notion. It allows us to discuss and explain how and why we are answering the question the way we are or why we are suggesting a tweak to their technique. It also allows you to get input from the students. It is also worth modelling the misconceptions that you have observed. This, coupled with seeing it modelled correctly, will support the students to understand why they need to try to replicate what you are modelling. Try using examples and non-examples to support students' learning. This involves showing students the correct way to perform a skill and modelling this explicitly, but also modelling a poorly performed skill while explaining why it is incorrect. For example, Louise Wallis-Tayler was teaching a Year 9 shooting lesson in basketball:

Louise had explained the key teaching points, going through the BEEF acronym (balance, eyes, elbow, follow-through), and modelled this to the students along with a breakdown of each step, questioning the students on each step. 'Why is this so important? What do I need to do to make sure I have a stable base and I am balanced? What is the purpose of the follow-through? Where should my eyes be looking?' A proportion of the students were shooting successfully in terms of scoring well throughout the practice. However, the students were shooting from the hip as opposed to above their heads. Louise modelled the correct technique again, followed by the incorrect technique that the students were displaying. She paused and asked the students to reflect on which one was going to be the most suitable in a game situation and why. While she gave the students time to think, she modelled both techniques again several times. The students were able to then understand how shooting from the hip is more likely to be blocked by an opponent in a game situation. Following her live modelling, the quality of students' understanding and performance in the skill both improved considerably.

This is also the case when modelling in theory lessons. Live modelling lends itself to opening discussions regarding metacognition and the implicit processes you go through with regards to planning, monitoring and evaluating your answers. When you're planning a model answer to an exam question, make sure to unpick and explore the following questions:

♦ What is the command word, and what is the question asking for (e.g. evaluate, discuss, analyse, justify)?

♦ What does each of the key terms mean?

- What key knowledge is required in order to answer the question?

- How are the marks divided up across the assessment objectives (AOs)?

- What AO1 knowledge am I going to be assessed on?

- What application do I need to ensure I cover when preparing my response to ensure I fulfil AO2? What do I know about that sport or activity?

- What does AO3 look like for this specific command word?

Let's look at an example of how to tackle the following exam question:

John is extremely tall and thin. His father is encouraging him to join a local basketball club. Evaluate whether or not basketball is a suitable activity for John to take part in. (6 marks)

Step 1. Box the command word, underline the key words and circle the number of marks. I do this to ensure that I know what the question is asking and am responding to the command word. I need to plan my answer correctly with an appropriate structure and show my knowledge of the content being assessed.

Step 2. Consider the command word. So, the command word is 'evaluate'. This requires me to judge from the available evidence. John being tall and thin leads to me think he is an ectomorph. *(How can we remember this? Well, the T in the word 'ectomorph' is a visual representation of the body shape of someone who is tall and thin. Like the D in 'endomorph' is a visual reminder of the shape of someone who has high body fat percentage. The M in 'mesomorph' is a reminder that the body type has a high muscle mass. This memory strategy leads me to think about the body shape of the ectomorph – long levers, tall and thin, low body fat and muscle mass, narrow shoulders and hips.)*

Step 3. Consider the sport. In basketball, as a sport, athletes would benefit from being tall due to being closer to the basket for shots, rebounds, blocks and tip-offs. However, John is thin as well as tall, so a counter-argument may be that low body fat and muscle could lead to less power or agility to drive, jump, dribble and move around the court efficiently.

Step 4. Consider the key words. We need to consider the key words and the key knowledge required to answer this question. The key words would be 'tall', 'thin', 'basketball' and 'suitable activity'. The key knowledge I need to think about is my understanding of how being tall and thin can be influential in basketball. Are there any elements of the sport that may not be suitable for someone who is tall and thin? Is the body type enough to ensure he can be successful in the sport? What other factors could impact his suitability – such as skill level, his desire to play basketball or other sports he may be more suited to?

Step 5. Break down the marks. So, there are 6 marks available here. AO1 = 1 mark for knowledge of somatotype, AO2 = 2 marks for the application of the performer to the sport (i.e. why the somatotype is useful in basketball), and AO3 = 3 marks for analysis/evaluation of John's suitability to the sport. This creates a checklist for me to refer back to while answering the question.

Step 6. Begin the response:

♦ John is predominantly an ectomorph body type, due to being described as tall and thin. *(This covers AO1 – tick that off of the checklist – AO2 is next.)*

♦ Ectomorphs are often seen playing basketball as height has a key benefit. Taller athletes will be closer to the height of the basket. They are also less likely to be blocked when shooting. *(I have given two different comments on John's suitability in the context of the sport, so I can tick off the 2 AO2 marks – and move on to my analysis for AO3.)*

♦ It is clear that John's height does provide a distinct advantage, including during shooting, blocking, tip-offs and rebounding. *(There is 1 AO3 mark.)* However, being tall is not enough to be successful on its own; John would need to be good at the skills required, such as dribbling, passing and defending. *(There is my second AO3 mark as I have started to create a judgement.)* Not all elite players are tall and thin, as power, strength, speed and agility are also crucial components to be successful in the sport. John may be better off adding some muscle bulk to his natural frame to increase his chance of success. *(There is the third AO3 mark. I am now going to reread my answer and double-check that I am happy with my response, amending if necessary.)*

When you are completing a model answer with the students, you can live model how you would use your monitoring strategies to ensure that your response is wholly appropriate. Live modelling, simply put, is when the teacher writes the answer to the question, pausing and stopping to ask questions such as: what should we do next? Why have I done that step? Why is that step next? You are showing what you are thinking: how you apply your cognition. The foundations of a successful answer will be built in the planning stage. Use a checklist to ensure that you have covered all the AOs while creating your response. Once you've created the model answer, you can resume acting as the PE teacher, sharing how you would evaluate the response, using a mark scheme to see where marks could be lost, explicitly referencing what might need to be done differently next time linked to the task, strategy and learner. Throughout this process, you are playing the role of both the learner and the teacher. The students need to be able to see how you are constructing the answer (as the learner) *and* understand how you are evaluating and grading it (as the teacher). Better yet, the students will gradually learn to act the part of the teacher by asking these questions of their own work and the processes they go through to create it.

Live modelling is equally effective if you reverse it – starting with the model answer and working back through the steps. Some questions to consider are:

♦ What are the key topics that we need to cover in this answer?

♦ What is the question asking us?

♦ How are we going to structure our response so we can achieve all three AOs?

♦ Why did we start the answer with that?

♦ What should we do next?

♦ What is the correct term to use to explain that concept?

♦ What do we mean when we say that in the response?

♦ What should we add to finish this section of the response?

♦ What have we missed from this part of the response?

♦ Have we used appropriate terminology?

Let's explore an example of how this might work for the same question:

John is extremely tall and thin. His father is encouraging him to join a local basketball club. Evaluate whether or not basketball is a suitable activity for John to take part in. (6 marks)

First, we would present the class with our model answer:

John is predominantly an ectomorph body type, due to being described as tall and thin. Ectomorphs are often seen playing basketball as height has a key benefit. Taller athletes will be closer to the height of the basket. They are also less likely to get blocked when shooting. It is clear that John's height does provide a distinct advantage, including during shooting, blocking, tip-offs and rebounding. However, being tall is not enough to be successful on its own; John would need to be good at the skills required, such as dribbling, passing and defending. Not all elite players are tall and thin, as strength, speed and agility are also crucial components to be successful in the sport. John may be better off adding some muscle bulk to his natural frame to increase his chance of success.

We would then deconstruct the answer with the class, using questioning to ensure that the students understand how and why we have arrived at it.

Teacher: What are the key topics that we covered in this answer … Olivia?

Olivia: Somatotypes and knowledge of basketball.

Teacher: Thank you. So what was the question asking us to do then … Ellie?

Ellie: It asks us to evaluate, which means we need to judge from available evidence.

Teacher: Perfect. So let's look at the structure of the response. Do we understand how the marks are going to be awarded … Muzamel?

Muzamel: It's a 6-mark question so should be 1 mark for AO1, 2 marks for AO2 and 3 marks for AO3.

Teacher: Excellent, Muzamel What does that mean for the structure that we used then … Marc?

Marc: It means you have 1 mark for the knowledge, 2 marks for applying it to the sport – in this question that is basketball – and 3 marks for the analysis or evaluation.

Teacher: Correct, Marc. So why did I start the answer with: 'John is predominantly an ectomorph body type, due to being described as tall and thin. Ectomorphs are often seen playing basketball as height has a key benefit. Taller athletes will be closer to the height of the basket. They are also less likely to get blocked when shooting.' … Summer?

Summer: Because that covers the AO1 mark by identifying that John is an ectomorph because he is tall and thin. It also covers the 2 AO2 marks as it applies his height to the sport and how it will impact the sport positively by linking the shooting bit in too.

Teacher: Yes, well done. What comes next in the structure then … Zach?

Zach: The AO3 parts?

Teacher: Yes, exactly. Where in the response are the AO3 marks addressed? Is there anything missing or that might need adding … Sienna?

Sienna: They do this by talking about how his height would help with shooting, rebounding and blocking.

Teacher: Would you agree … Josh?

Josh: Yes, but I do think they could add in that power would be needed to jump even higher.

Teacher: Brilliant, Josh. That would add a further potential AO3 mark. What do we think enables this response to pick up the final AO3 marks on offer … Izzy?

Izzy: I think by offering the argument about skills being influential and then linking other components of fitness, it balances the discussion about his height being important but not the only factor. They then provide a good closing sentence and add the judgement that's needed in an 'evaluate' question when they say: 'Not all elite players are tall and thin, as power, strength, speed and agility are also crucial components to be successful in the sport. John may be better off adding some muscle bulk to his natural frame to increase his chance of success.'

Teacher: Brilliant. Well done, Izzy.

Live modelling is key to developing a strong understanding of practical activities and equipping students with the skills to make informed decisions on how to apply their knowledge to a variety of scenarios. It is more than just showing students the finished article; it is about deconstructing it by discussing the thinking and the processes which will get them there. It is also a powerful way of promoting effective questioning, as can be seen from the prompts.

So, the next time you model a tackle in rugby, don't just expect students to emulate it; show them the processes to go through, get them to see, understand and respect the importance of the how and the why. The same can be said for 6- and 9-mark exam questions: make explicit all of the processes you go through to get to that final response, questioning the students on the what, the how and the why or why not. My colleague, Ryan De Gruchy, explains it as follows:

I found that all too often I was going straight to showing the answer and simply talking students through it. My students struggled to access the top marks of the longer-answer questions. This was due to not spending enough time discussing how to plan the answer. I then changed my practice and instead projected the exam question on the whiteboard. I then annotate my thoughts, discussing each logical step I take with the students in order to support them with being able to do this more independently over time.

We use the box, circle, underline method. The process itself involves boxing the command word – this leads to thinking about the response required by that specific word (e.g. 'discuss' means 'talk or write about (a topic) in detail, taking into account different issues or ideas', while 'evaluate' means 'form an idea of the amount, number, or value of; assess.'[4] In student-friendly terms 'discuss' means 'give positives and negatives', whereas 'evaluate' means 'provide a judgement

---

4   According to the Google dictionary, provided by Oxford Languages.

from the evidence available to you'. We underline the key words, such as the tier 2 or 3 terminology and the sport, asking ourselves 'What do I know about that sport, and what do the key words mean in this context?' Finally, we circle the number of marks so we know how many marks there are for AO1, AO2 and AO3. This also creates a handy checklist to use when modelling the answer. For an AQA 6-mark question, there would be 1 mark for demonstrating the knowledge (AO1) – usually definitions of the key words – 2 marks for the application to the sport (AO2) and then 3 marks for the specific command word responses (AO3). I live model this to students several times. We create some answers together, and I ask them questions to reveal their thinking at each step along the journey. Then, finally, they complete the metacognitive planning strategy on their own. So far this has led students to be more aware of how to answer the questions and what structure to use, leading to more students being able to apply their knowledge and access the top grade band.

In this example, Ryan uses metacognitive live modelling to make his implicit processes, as the expert, explicit to his students. The box, circle, underline method provides students with a strategy they can use to bridge the gap between their knowledge and successfully using and applying it as directed by complex exam questions. One of the reasons why this is a successful technique to use is that it breaks down all of the information that students need in order to answer the question. It shows them the steps to go through and alleviates the sense of doom and the feeling of not knowing where to begin. An example of this is on page 69.

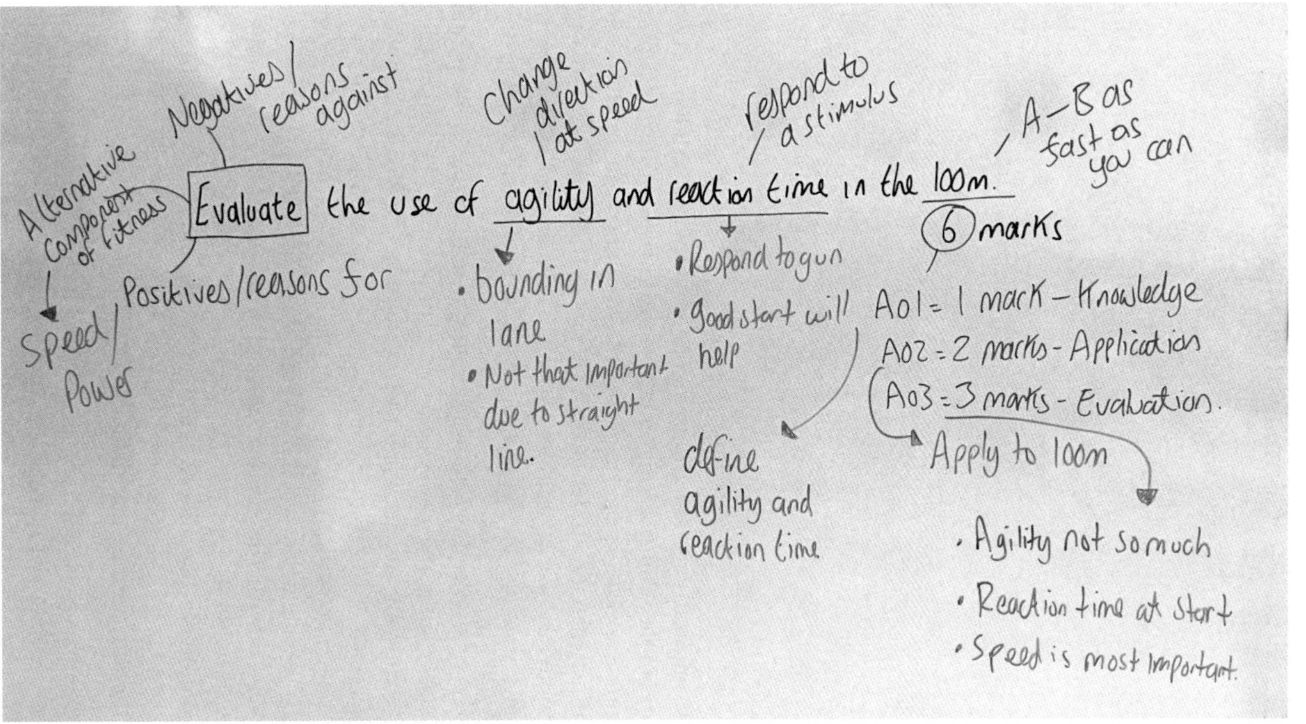

Alternative component of fitness
Negatives / reasons against
Positives / reasons for
Speed / Power

Evaluate the use of agility and reaction time in the 100m.
6 marks

Change direction / at speed
respond to / a stimulus
A—B as fast as you can

• bounding in lane
• Not that important due to straight line.

• Respond to gun
• good start will help

define agility and reaction time

AO1 = 1 mark — Knowledge
AO2 = 2 marks — Application
AO3 = 3 marks — Evaluation.
Apply to 100m

• Agility not so much
• Reaction time at start
• Speed is most important.

2. Comparative Modelling

Comparative modelling involves showing students two examples – one strong and one weak. If we are shown only one example, it can be quite difficult to critique it. However, if we provide students with the opportunity to compare one model answer to another, we make it much easier for them to pick out the strengths and weaknesses of each one.

For example, if we showed students an example of someone performing the swivel hips in trampolining, in which they technically did perform two seat drops facing in opposite directions, but they brought their legs around to the side, they may initially think that the execution is pretty good. However, when we show them the same skill performed at height with the correct upward rotational half twist, they will begin to spot the weaknesses in the first example. They should also be able to see that the second example is better because of the increased height, the correct half twist and the two perfect seat drops.

Comparative modelling is essential for encouraging students to critique with precision so they can then use the perfect model to shape their own performance. This is said to be true in theory settings as well. Using two different responses to the same question and encouraging healthy discussion over key strengths and weaknesses will support the students when it comes to creating their own answers. To show the students what is wrong with a piece of writing, they need to compare it to something better. So an example for a 4-mark multi-stage fitness test (MSFT) question might be:

Discuss the appropriateness of the multi-stage fitness test for a marathon runner. (4 marks)

Student A – The multi-stage fitness test is relevant for marathons as it measures cardiovascular endurance. You need this to last for the whole race and prevent fatigue. It also gets harder like a marathon would.

Student B – The multi-stage fitness test (MSFT) is relevant for a marathon runner as it measures cardiovascular endurance. This, along with muscular endurance, is important to maintain performance levels for the whole race. However, due to the shuttles only being 20 metres and involving changes in direction, it could be argued that the movements don't replicate the race. This is also the case with the constant increases in intensity as the MSFT is progressive.

In this example, student A has only identified the positives, misinterpreted the command word of 'discuss' and hasn't linked the test to the sport, meaning they would only pick up 1 mark. In comparison, student B has given both positives and negatives of the test and discussed its relevance to the sport.

3. Say It Back to Me

Having shown students how to perform a skill or complete a task and unpicking it with them, we should check that they really understand how to do it before we let them loose, pre-empting the classic question 'What are we supposed to be doing, Sir?' To avoid that confusion and any uncertainty around our expectations regarding the task, we can simply ask students to repeat the instructions back to us. We can do this through Doug Lemov's *Teach Like a Champion* strategy of cold calling (directing questioning at specific students, rather than asking the class to volunteer responses), and not using a student's name until after we have paused at the end of our question.[5] For example:

So, what is the first thing you are going to do when you get to your court? … We will start with you, Mandy.

Thank you, Mandy. When do we change the person serving … Lizzie?

Thank you, Lizzie. Why are we rotating the serve in this task … Lauren?

---

4. Worked Examples in Theory and Practical

Simply put, worked examples are a completed example labelled with the steps needed. Ideally, this then leads to students partially completing examples themselves until the examples are faded away and students can perform the skill with increasing independence. Worked examples are useful in supporting students as they can refer back to them when tackling future problems, as long as they are tethered to

---

5   Doug Lemov, *Teach Like a Champion: 49 Techniques that Put Students on the Path to College* (San Francisco, CA: Jossey-Bass, 2010).

information the students already hold in their long-term memory. As they become more confident with the approach, they will become less dependent on the worked example, but at the novice stage they can serve as a good model. In PE theory, the use of worked examples for things like Ryan's 6-marker box, circle, underline method is relatively self-explanatory. Allowing students to use worked examples, or partially worked examples, as scaffolds requires thought and consideration regarding the level of challenge. We are aiming for support rather than overreliance. You should ask yourself:

♦ How will I ensure that the worked example offers the opportunity to extend thinking and is not too restrictive?

♦ Does the worked example still require students to think?

♦ How will I ensure that the worked example is fit for purpose and not impeding learning?

♦ How will I know that the students are in the struggle zone and not the comfort zone with regards to challenge?

♦ When should the worked example be removed?

Worked examples are most effective when they have been created with student input. This has the added advantage of supporting their self-efficacy and ensures that the resources are at the appropriate level for the students in the room. To be effective, worked examples must be similar to the problem that the students are trying to solve. If you want them to evaluate, they will need a worked example that demonstrates how to do so.

In practical lessons, worked examples are much trickier to use. The obvious barrier is that students cannot hold the mental image of your live modelled skill in their heads indefinitely. We can use students to model (if their technique suffices) as this will support the self-efficacy of other students in the group. However, the question still remains: how can we support students to use our worked example as a scaffold within their own performance? In an increasingly technologically advanced world, the answer is at our finger-tips: video analysis. Most students have mobile phones, which will allow them to view and replay video clips. You can film the perfect model performing a skill or activity, play it in slow motion, and this can be used as a worked example, with careful commentary on each successful step, to support students in the same way as a written model in their books does in theory lessons. We can use this to support students with understanding their own misconceptions, showing them a perfect model alongside their own videoed perfor-mance, allowing them to see first hand where they can improve. Technology allows us to use comparative model-ling in our practical lessons with ease. For example, when teaching the swivel hips in trampolining, the teacher could model the skill or show a video clip (e.g. YouTube) and then the students could film their partner performing the skill. Students could then watch their performance back in slow motion and physically see the mistakes they are making compared to the perfect model.

5. Modelling Composite Parts
of the Complex Problem

More often than not, when students are unsuccessful at a specific skill it is down to a very small technical change that will transform the output. For example, when learning to serve in badminton, some students struggle to make contact with the shuttlecock. With a slight tweak – usually to the length of the racket, how they are holding the shuttlecock or getting them to stop lifting the shuttlecock – the issue can be rectified. To prevent this becoming a mainstay in our les-sons, we need to break down the complex actions we are trying to teach into smaller, more manageable, composite parts. For example, in the badminton serving example, you would first model the grip of the racket, then how to hold the shuttlecock, how to stand and transfer your weight, then the drop of the shuttlecock while moving the racket towards the point of contact. We model each of those composite parts, providing students with the opportunity to practise each of them before putting them all together. This will be explored further during Chapters 4 and 5.

Reflective Questions

♦ Are you confident enough across all activities to model the key skills to students?

♦ Are you confident enough to model all of your implicit thought processes live on the whiteboard?

♦ Are you confident enough to metacognitively model the how and why in practical lessons?

♦ Do you model how and how not to complete skills in practical lessons, linked to students' misconceptions?

♦ Do you use students' exemplary work and critique it as a class?

♦ Do you scaffold your modelling and questioning at each stage to support students' learning?

♦ Do you ask students to repeat instructions back to you prior to starting a task?

♦ How do you use worked examples in your practical lessons?

Chapter 4
Practice

The second of Rosenshine's principles of instruction is: 'Present new material in small steps, with student practice after each step.'[1] Our first thought regarding practice should be, do we offer sufficient time and opportunity for our students to practise? We can be, at times, too keen to move students on. Seeing them perform a well-timed forehand groundstroke in tennis, we immediately think, 'Brilliant, how can I move them on?' This is also evident in theory teaching: a student answers a few questions on altitude training and we think, 'Brilliant, let's move on to spectator behaviour.' The effect of this is that we skip the practice and replace it with more new content. The problem this creates is that students do not get the opportunity, as Rosenshine suggests, to work with newly encountered knowledge, understand it and store it for future use. This then leads to content being forgotten in theory lessons and skills being underdeveloped in practical lessons. Daniel Willingham suggests that students need to devote an additional 20% of the time that it took them to master a new concept in order to embed understanding and secure retention long term.[2] We need to provide students with extra practice before moving on.

Shaun Allison and Andy Tharby propose that we think of practice in two distinct ways:

1   *Practice for fluency – so that we achieve automaticity.*

2   *Deliberate practice – so that we practise at the outer reaches of our ability (purposeful practice).*[3]

---

1   Rosenshine, Principles of Instruction, p. 12.
2   Daniel T. Willingham, What Will Improve a Student's Memory? *American Educator* (winter 2008–2009): 17–25 at 22. Available at: https://www.aft.org/sites/default/files/willingham_0.pdf.
3   Allison and Tharby, *Making Every Lesson Count*, pp. 126–127.

Fluency refers to students having knowledge and procedures so well understood in their long-term memory that they can be recalled or performed effortlessly. Therefore, it will not impact on the students' working memory and cognitive load, allowing them to deal more successfully with the knowledge being encountered for the first time. For example, when a novice receives a pass in football, they are working hard on understanding the speed, height and angle of the pass, thinking about which part of the foot to stop the ball with and how to keep it close to them, their eyes fixated on the travelling ball. Once they have achieved this to automaticity, they will not be thinking about any of those things; it will appear natural. They will then have space in their working memory to think about how they are going to play a first-time pass to a teammate who has made an intelligent run. They can begin to tether the decision-making element of football to their schemata of how to control and pass the ball, as this prior knowledge has been practised and is now fluent. It is important in PE that we give our students time to practise for fluency.

Purposeful practice is the vehicle we use to ensure our students are challenged and pushed to the outer reaches of their capability. The nuance of purposeful practice lies in knowing how involved to be as the teacher. This is shown on the continuum on page 79.[4]

Knowing where you are on this continuum is class dependent and, specifically, dependent on the individual students you are teaching, as well as the unit or topic. The continuum provides a useful starting point and will be delved into in greater depth throughout this chapter.

---

4 Allison and Tharby, *Making Every Lesson Count*, p. 128.

Dependence	Heavy guidance	Light guidance	Independence	Autonomy
Teacher explains and models new content. Students are predominantly listening, watching and taking notes.	Teacher leads practice through questioning, discussion and supports. Cognitive work is shared with the teacher.	Students are doing cognitive work on their own with regular teacher feedback and fewer supports.	Students work with and apply new knowledge for an extended period of time without the teacher's support. All cognitive work has now been passed to the student.	Students fluently manipulate knowledge and skills independently by applying them to new contexts.

It's clear to see how practice is a hugely essential part of the learning process. However, it's not quite as straightforward as simply doing something over and over again. We need to consider the following:

♦ **Practice makes permanent, not perfect.** Simply practising something again and again will not make students good at something; it will just make it stick. For example, students could be answering lots of questions on the health and other benefits of physical activity; however, if they are doing it wrong, they will just continue to do it badly. This is the same in practical lessons too. If students keep practising batting with an incorrect grip, they will just embed bad habits.

♦ **Repetition is key.** In order to memorise something, we need to come back to it time and time again and practise retrieving it from memory. The process of retrieval helps to strengthen and speed up our memory. This is potentially quite tricky in practical lessons due to spacing. This is also the case in theory lessons due to the increased demand from the new specification regarding content. Homework can become a valuable tool to support this.

♦ **Interleaving and spacing.** Cognitive science suggests that to optimise learning we should switch between topics while we are studying them and make links between them.[5] Alongside this, we should allow some forgetting time between topics and return to them a few weeks later.

♦ **Is the practice fit for purpose?** The pitfall we often stumble into as PE teachers is that we judge the impact of our practice by asking a few follow-up questions at the end of the lesson and then use that information to determine whether or not the students have learnt what we intended. This is due to the fact that we tend to teach a topic in a lesson or a skill in a practical lesson. It is then only revisited the following year or the next time that sport is taught.

---

5 Perry et al., *Cognitive Science Approaches in the Classroom.*

♦ **Practice should keep them in the struggle zone.** The importance of the struggle zone was discussed in Chapter 1. If practice is going to be productive, we need to ensure that students are working in the struggle zone. If they are practising within their comfort zone, they will not be getting better.

Practice Strategies

1. Parameters of Practice (Practically)

PE teachers will often use a single lesson to introduce or develop a specific skill linked to a physical activity or sport. For example, to develop the dig in volleyball you may start with an explanation of the dig, potentially probing the students to check their understanding. This is typically followed with a few models of the dig, showing the students the key points of the technique and highlighting common misconceptions and what they need to avoid. The students will then have time to practise the skill in isolation. The teacher may give some feedback to support this. The class will then move on to looking at the skill in a more challenging situation, potentially over the net or following a serve. Again, the teacher may question students to generate deeper thinking or may provide some feedback. Invariably, the lesson then finishes with a game. The parameters of this game can either create a real opportunity for the students to hone their development, understanding and execution of the skill, including the decision-making element, or it can be directionless: the focus of the lesson is lost and students play as they always have, without any real focus on the core objective of developing the dig.

In order to ensure that our game play is effective practice and explicitly linked to the lesson objective, we need to encourage students to use the skills they have been practising within the game. There are a multitude of ways in which we can do this. In the volleyball example, we can insist on players using a dig every time the ball crosses the net or give 2 points if the dig leads to a successful set and spike, thus encouraging setting up the point correctly. We could also start the game with a throw to someone who must dig the ball. All we are doing is creating more opportunities for students to practise the skill while introducing the competitive element of game play. This can also be the case when looking at a broader topic or game principle. For example, when looking at the use of width when attacking in football, rather than simply playing a game with two central goals at either end of the pitch, you could have two goals per team near the corner flags, encouraging the teams to transfer the ball from side to side if one goal has been shut off by defenders. You could also have wide channels in which the attacker cannot be tackled. Both examples are 'games' but are encouraging and providing more opportunities to use the focus of the lesson: width when attacking.

2. Retrieval Practice

'Retrieval practice' is a term coined by cognitive scientists.[6] It essentially involves finding opportunities for students to think about topics by retrieving them from memory. In simple terms, there are two types of memory: working memory and long-term memory. Long-term memory is an infinite storehouse of information we can retrieve and use without

---

6   Perry et al., *Cognitive Science Approaches in the Classroom.*

thinking too deeply about it; it will always be there and can be retrieved when required. For example, if you are of a certain age, you will remember your home phone number from when you were a child despite not having thought about it for years. The reason you can remember this is because you had to retrieve and use it so many times; this will never be forgotten as it will always be stored in your long-term memory. Whereas working memory is the space in which we use and think about new information. Individuals can typically hold five to nine pieces of information in their working memory at any one time.[7] The main aim of retrieval practice is to support the transfer of information into the infinite storehouse of our long-term memory to allow us more thinking capacity in our working memory. This can, at times, prove a bit tricky due to the large amount of content in the GCSE curriculum. There is obviously a fine line here between taking up too much curriculum time and creating ample opportunities for students to think back, thus supporting the retention of the content longer term. The information can provide the teacher and the students with invaluable insights about gaps in knowledge, which can be used to support future curriculum planning, or content can be immediately retaught to prevent misconceptions becoming embedded. There are many forms of retrieval practice; the key is that the information be retrieved from memory, not from looking back in books. John Dunlosky highlights the importance of students recalling information from their long-term memory in enhancing and securing learning.[8]

Low-stakes quizzing is one vehicle that can be used. The key notion here is that the quizzing should be low stakes. Daniel Willingham suggests that 'memory is the residue of thought'.[9] In the same way as our Year 9s can reel off masses

---

7   Miller, The Magical Number Seven, Plus or Minus Two.

8   John Dunlosky, Strengthening the Student Toolbox: Study Strategies to Boost Learning, *American Educator*, 37(3) (2013): 12–21 at 13. Available at: https://files.eric.ed.gov/fulltext/EJ1021069.pdf

9   Daniel T. Willingham, *Why Don't Students Like School? A Cognitive Scientist Answers Questions About How the Mind Works and What It Means for the Classroom* (San Francisco, CA: Jossey-Bass, 2010), p. 54.

of statistics about their favourite footballer, students remember what they think about. Our role, therefore, is to create opportunities for students to think deeply about what they have done, are doing and are going to do in lessons. Low-stakes quizzing is a way to promote this thinking in theory lessons. Having a quiz on previously taught content at the start of a lesson will encourage students to model the thinking that we are seeking. An example quiz structure follows.

Possible Quiz Structure

Questions 1–3: retrieve key knowledge from last lesson.

Question 4: retrieve key knowledge from last week.

Question 5: retrieve key knowledge from last term.

Question 6: retrieve key knowledge from last lesson and connect it to knowledge from last term.

1   What is the lever system in operation at the ankle when taking off in long jump?

2   Draw and label a third-class lever system.

3   How do you work out mechanical advantage?

4   What is the plane of motion and axis of rotation at the shoulder when performing a cartwheel?

5   What is the definition of power? Give a sporting example of when you would require power.

6   Identify the components of fitness in action, the plane of motion, axes of rotation, agonist muscle and lever system at the elbow when executing a chest pass in netball.

In this example, the topic from last lesson is lever systems, the topic from last week is planes and axes and last term's topic is components of fitness. Following this quiz, the teacher would go through the answers with the students, asking questions so they can make an informed decision about what to do next in terms of future planning. The teacher would provide immediate feedback or address any shared misconceptions. The results would not be shared or collected in, keeping the exercise low stakes. Another effective way to use retrieval practice is with homework; this can be done through setting questions relating to topics from last week or last term. It can also be done through having a lag on the homework, meaning the homework is always on previously taught topics. An example of a two-week lag follows.

Week	Lesson topic	Homework topic
1	Heart and cardiac cycle	Training types (taught last term)
2	Pathway of air	Aerobic and anaerobic respiration (taught last term)
3	Spirometry, link to exercise	Heart and cardiac cycle
4	Blood doping	Pathway of air
5	Performance-enhancing drugs (PEDs)	Spirometry, link to exercise
6	Hooliganism and spectator behaviour	Blood doping

In our subject, there are many ways in which we can support the principle of retrieval practice. I have tried to synthesise some of these here:

♦ **Write 100 questions for every topic you teach.** Make sure to include the answers, as this will eliminate any chance of inconsistency or misconception. These can then be adapted in lots of ways to support the students.

♦ **Mind maps or brain dumps from memory.** Give students a key topic or question and get them to write down as much information as they can from memory. You can also do this using mini whiteboards in practical lessons.

♦ **Blank knowledge organisers.** These will be explained in strategy 6 on page 94. Briefly, they can be used to test retrieval by providing headings and getting students to fill in the blanks.

♦ **Memory means memory.** Retrieval practice must be done from memory. Students should not be afforded any time to look back at their notes or discuss topics prior to completing the quiz or retrieval activity.

♦ **Revision strategy.** Flashcards are an essential and effective revision strategy. The common myth among students is that making and reading them is enough. In order for them to actually be useful, they should pose a question on the front and then have the answer on the back. They are used to pose those questions, students then verbalise or write down the answer before checking if they were correct, thus retrieving the answer from their memory.

♦ **Homework should include retrieval.** As previously outlined, homework should include retrieval tasks to support the strategy of thinking from memory. Obviously, we cannot ensure that students do this from memory at home. However, by shifting the focus of the homework away from raw scores to supporting students in identifying areas of development, we can alleviate some of the unnecessary pressure on getting the answers right whatever the cost.

3. Scaffolding

As PE teachers, we can all think of a lesson where some students were flying and had mastered the skill or concept that we were teaching to the point of being able to select and apply their knowledge in a complex full-context scenario. In that same lesson, we can probably all picture that student who is still struggling with very basic elements of the skill or concept; the mere thought of them being able to complete the skill under any pressure seems a world away. The challenge this presents us with is not unique and is one we seem to face as a daily occurrence.

Scaffolding is the way in which we construct our support and then gradually remove it at the right time. Knowing when to do this will be dependent upon the students and this is ultimately the art of differentiation. Some of the strategies we can use to scaffold effectively are as follows:

- **Model, model again and model some more.** Before adding the scaffold, we should show the students what they are aiming for. This will ensure that they are aware of the process to go through and have an understanding of how the skill or concept can be achieved and why we are practising it. We can show worked examples in theory lessons and also in practical lessons, if you have access to video equipment.

- **Intervene.** A robust scaffold may be the best strategy for some students, while others will just need a slight tweak or a nudge. This can sometimes take the form of a verbal suggestion, 'Try opening up the angle of the racket face', or a subtle tweak to their equipment, moving the racket up and behind their head to show them the ready position. For others, this requires some wider unpicking through elaborative questioning or stripping back the practice to refocus their technique.

- **Atomisation.** As we move towards the more complex skills or starting to put more variable elements into our lessons — such as answering 6- and 9-mark exam questions or breaking down an organised defence in football — we need to be mindful of each step and ensure that students have the opportunity to practise it. We need to cover the what, how and why, providing feedback where required along the way. The art here is to use the scaffold to support students while encouraging them to be thinking on their own about the best way to use the skill or concept in an unpredictable game or exam.

♦ **Remove the scaffolding.** When we learn how to swim as children, we may use armbands until we are ready to remove them. We only intend to use them for as long as is necessary. It is the same with PE teaching; the aim of the scaffolds we use is to remove them to allow the students to flourish. The difficulty is in knowing when the time is right to strip the scaffolding back. In my experience, this comes with understanding your students and not making assumptions about what they know and can do. In essence, I would suggest stripping the support back, as we can always put the armbands back on if we find that we need to.

4. Make the Links, and Make Them Explicit

All of our practical activities and theory topics have cross-overs that link them together. For example, we teach passing, shooting, defending, width, height and depth in football and in handball. In theory lessons, we teach technology and how it can improve player performance and support officials in making the correct decisions. This links to commercialisation and how the golden triangle (the financial relationship between sports, sponsors and the media) can generate income to develop technology. We need to, firstly, identify these links and, secondly, make them explicit to students.

The hinge point of this is making the links explicit to students, getting them to think about other topics and find the connections. A good time to do this is at the end of a lesson. Too often, PE teachers use the question 'What have we learnt this lesson?' Not only is this a measure of performance and not learning – as learning is complex and takes time – but it does not promote thinking, which is one of the main purposes of a question. Instead, try 'What have we done in previous lessons that could link to what we have done today?' How to do this effectively will be discussed in Chapter 5.

5. Exam Questions

Usain Bolt is, at the time of writing, the world record holder for the 100m and 200m sprint. He worked hard and refined his craft through a rigorous training regime. A vital part of his training would be running the full length of the race, but also breaking the race down and working on specific stages, such as the start, acceleration and stride phases. Similarly, PE teachers should use mock exams and questions from past papers as part of their lessons to support students with the final exams. The best PE teachers will embed deconstructing and answering exam questions into their everyday practice. A simple process to go through when using exam questions is as follows:

1   Recap the knowledge students need to access the question.

2   Metacognitively plan the question if it's a higher-mark question and has multiple steps, being explicit about each step, the thinking and the why behind it.

3   Complete the question.

4   Go through the answer – focusing on key misconceptions and terminology. This can be done by working through a model answer or a student's answer, drawing comparisons with the students' work. At this stage, you could allow peer or self-marking as well as the more traditional route of teacher marking.

5   Work through the misconceptions, showing students how and where they went wrong. Always make sure students amend their responses to address any necessary corrections or improvements.

6   Answer another, similar, question to reinforce the correct response (avoiding the misconceptions).

As an example, let's take the exam question:

Evaluate the use of agility and reaction time in the 100m sprint. (6 marks)

The first thing to do would be to check the students' understanding of the components of fitness cited in the question, including definitions and changing context across different sports. Then begin the explicit process of unpicking the thought processes you, as the expert, will go through when preparing to answer this question: understanding the command word, the sport and how the marks are to be awarded. Talk aloud to yourself, narrating your thoughts to the students. Give the students six minutes to answer the question in exam conditions – in silence, on their own. During this stage, the teacher would circulate and gain a picture of what the common misconceptions are or where students are dropping marks. The teacher will then address the root cause of the misconceptions and ensure students are aware of the pitfalls they may have fallen into. The issue may be with their understanding of the content or their exam technique, but both can be worked on and improved. The teacher will then provide a similar question worth the same number of marks, changing the components of fitness and the sport but keeping the command word the same. They then repeat the process of coaching the students in how to approach the question, allowing them time to answer, and working through the misconceptions.

For our example question, the process might look something like this:

Step 1. Check students' understanding of the components of fitness, including definitions and changing context across different sports as well as the 100m. Use questioning, for example:

- What do we understand by the term 'reaction time'?
- What do we understand by the term 'agility'?
- What are the correct definitions?
- Can you think of an example of agility from any sport?
- Can you think of an example of reaction time from any sport?
- Will you need agility in the 100m? If so, where? If not, why not?
- Will you need reaction time in the 100m? If so, where? If not, why not?
- Are there any other components of fitness that may be deemed more important in the 100m? Why?

Check students' understanding of the command word and the structure required to answer the question.

♦ What does the command word 'evaluate' mean?

♦ What will that mean for the structure?

♦ How many marks are available for AO1, AO2 and AO3?

♦ What do we need to do in terms of the structure of our answer to ensure that we get all of the marks on offer?

Step 2. The teacher then explains how to structure the question and what the answer needs, narrating each step of the journey and explaining the why. This will be done using the responses the students provided in the previous step.

♦ Include the definitions of the two components of fitness identified in the question. This ensures you get the AO1 mark.

♦ Identify whether or not you need agility and reaction time in the 100m. This ensures you get the 2 AO2 marks available.

♦ Provide an argument explaining why reaction time is crucial. Clarify why agility is not fundamental and then explain that speed is likely to be the most important component of fitness because of the length of the race.

Step 3. The students now have all the information they need to complete their own answers, which they can do in silence while the teacher circulates.

Step 4. Go through the answer. The teacher might show a model answer – for example:

Agility is the ability to change direction quickly, while maintaining control. Reaction time is the time taken to initiate a response to a stimulus.

In the 100m, reaction time would be of significant importance in response to the gun to ensure you get a good start. Agility, on the other hand, would not be that important as the race is run in a straight line and therefore requires little change of direction.

If the athlete were to change direction and move out of the lane, this would result in disqualification. The performer may need minimal amounts of agility to alter their position in their own lane or when bounding out of the blocks. Reaction time is more important as the 100m sprint is the shortest outdoor sprint. Therefore, reaction time is usually crucial to success. Having said that, I do feel that speed is more important than both agility and reaction time.

They would examine this using the modelling strategies outlined in Chapter 3, requiring the students to compare and contrast with their own work.

Step 5. Explore misconceptions, correct the work, and discuss why you are doing so.

♦ Students often use the word 'react' when defining reaction time. Why is the word 'respond' so important here?

♦ The students will often neglect the command word, so this will need to be reiterated. How should we structure our response to ensure we 'evaluate' and do not 'discuss' or 'analyse'?

♦ Some students will have limited athletics knowledge and will need reminding that the 100m is not run on a bend and does not involve turning. How is the 100m race run? Do we run from A to B in a straight line, or does it involve changes in direction?

♦ As reaction time is crucial, some students will suggest that it is the most important component of fitness in the 100m. A useful way to tackle this is by identifying how poorly Usain Bolt started his race (due to poor reaction time) during his world-record-breaking run of 9.58 seconds at the 2009 World Championships in Berlin. The reason why he still won the race and broke the world record was due to his superior speed. Therefore, it could be argued that speed is *the* crucial factor in a successful 100m sprint.

Step 6. Answer another 'evaluate' question but with a different context. For example:

Evaluate the use of agility and strength in the javelin. (6 marks)

At this point, the teacher can remove some of the initial scaffolding and ask the students to answer independently (effectively beginning at step 3 of this sequence).

6. Knowledge Organisers

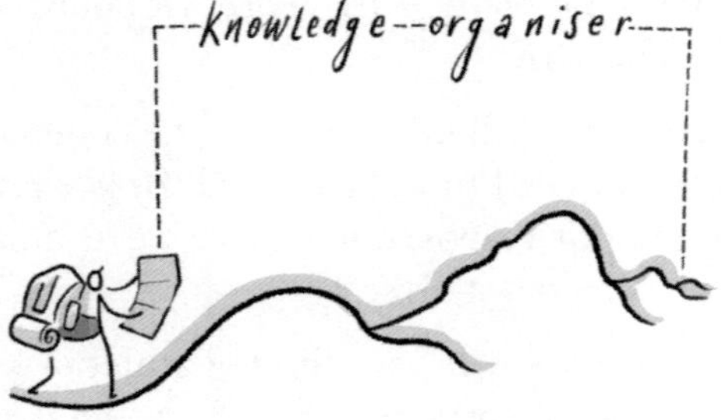

Joe Kirby defines a knowledge organiser in a very impassioned manner.[10] A knowledge organiser is an excellent

---

10 Joe Kirby, Knowledge Organisers, *Pragmatic Education* [blog] (28 March 2015). Available at: https://pragmaticreform.wordpress.com/2015/03/28/knowledge-organisers/.

starting point to get all of the knowledge you want students to know and practise using on one piece of paper. Essentially, they contain all of the key information, including diagrams or graphs, that you, as the teacher, deem vital for the students to know on a specific topic. For example, the knowledge organiser on pages 96–97 is an extract from AQA GCSE PE unit 3.1.1.2: The structure and functions of the cardio-respiratory system.

Knowledge organisers are a really useful retrieval practice tool. Students can be given copies with only the headings, so they can see how much of the key information they can retrieve from memory to fill in the blanks. They can be used as a scaffold to support students when practising answering exam questions. Another use could be as a checklist to see where students' knowledge gaps are. This can be through the form of testing or simply for students to gauge their understanding of what elements they were confident in or not. Tasks involving them as a knowledge retrieval tool could be set as homework. They could also be used to make flashcards to support home learning – parents could even use them to test their child.

A key feature is that the content in them is agreed as the core knowledge that it is fundamental for students to know in order to succeed in that specific unit. As such, they can really help to achieve coherence in planning within the department. They do take time to create, but, if used correctly, can support students in and beyond the classroom.

The structure and functions of the cardio-respiratory system

Cardiac output (Q)	Stroke volume (SV)	Heart rate (HR)
The amount of blood ejected from the heart in one minute OR stroke volume x heart rate.	The volume of blood pumped out of the heart during one contraction.	The number of times the heart beats per minute.

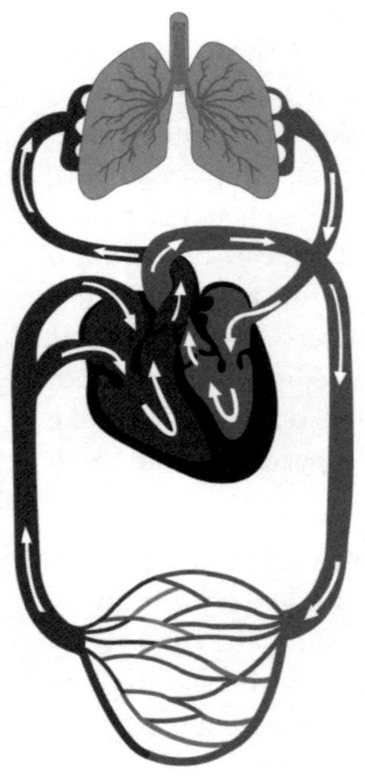

Cardiac Cycle
1 Deoxygenated blood enters the right side of the heart via the **vena cava**.
2 Heart contracts and pumps blood to the lungs via the **pulmonary artery**.
3 Blood becomes oxygenated in the **lungs**.
4 Oxygenated blood returns to the heart via the **pulmonary vein** and fills the left side.
5 Heart contracts and pumps blood to the body via the **aorta** to deliver oxygen.
6 Deoxygenated blood returns to the heart.

Cardiac cycle
The cardiac cycle is the repeated contraction and relaxation of the heart. There are two phases: diastole and systole.

Redistribution of blood	Example	Vasoconstriction	Vasodilation
When you exercise, the working muscles need more oxygen. When you exercise, heart rate and stroke volume increase. Blood is diverted away from inactive areas to the working muscles.	During exercise, blood can be redistributed away from the stomach (digestive system) to the working muscles.	Blood vessels are constricted (squeezed) to make them smaller/narrower. Blood flow reduced to these areas.	Blood vessels are dilated to make them bigger/wider. Blood flow to these areas increased. Supplies more oxygen and nutrients.

Blood vessels	Arteries	Veins	Capillaries
Structure	Thick muscular and elastic walls. Small lumen (internal diameter).	Thin walls. Contain valves to prevent backflow. Large lumen (internal diameter).	Very thin walls (one cell thick). Small lumen (internal diameter).
Functions	Carry blood at high pressure away from heart. Carry oxygenated blood (except the pulmonary artery). Used in redistribution of blood.	Carry blood at low pressure towards the heart. Carry deoxygenated blood (except the pulmonary vein).	Allow gaseous exchange – very thin walls allow oxygen and carbon dioxide to pass through. Link smaller arteries with smaller veins. Carry blood at low pressure.

Changes in heart rate before and during exercise
Before: Increase in heart rate – this is called the **anticipatory rise** – due to release of adrenaline.
During exercise: Muscles need more oxygen, which the blood transports. Cardiac output increases by increasing heart rate and/or stroke volume.

Diastole	Systole (S = squeezes)
When the chamber relaxes and fills with blood.	When the chamber contracts and ejects blood.

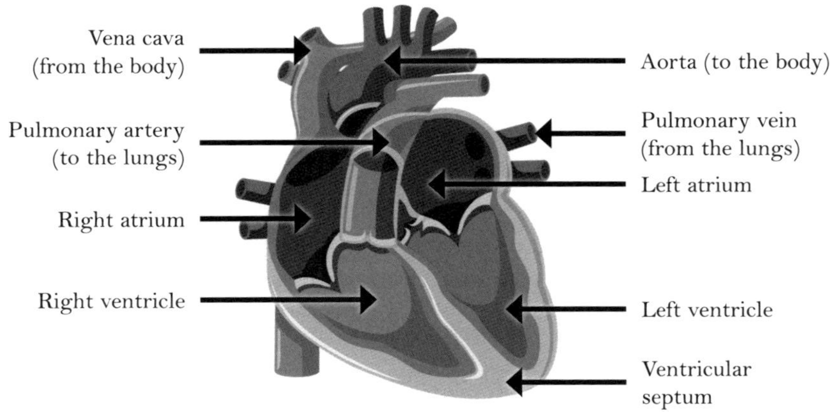

7. Overlearn

Daniel Willingham uses the phrase 'overlearning'. He suggests that even once we have learnt something and can recall it with confidence, we should continue to practise it so that it becomes automatic.[1] Lebron James won't stop practising free throws even though he has mastered the skill. He will continue to practise, so when he gets a free throw in a game, his routine will be automatic. This is much easier to implement in practical lessons, ensuring students get lots of opportunities to practise and refine their skills in specific tasks. With a lot of content to get through in GCSE PE, this can prove challenging. What follows are some points to consider:

♦ Use homework to overlearn topics that have already been covered in lessons.

♦ Give students lots of opportunities to complete exam questions, recapping and revisiting previous topics even when they have moved on to new ones.

♦ Identify core knowledge, such as the components of fitness in Paper 1. Take every opportunity to overlearn these topics. Include them in retrieval quizzes and verbally question students on them whenever they link to current topics.

---

1   Willingham, *What Will Improve a Student's Memory?*

Reflective Questions

♦ Do you set up tasks and game-related practices to provide opportunities for students to practise the key focus of that lesson?

♦ Do you monitor the practice students are doing so as not to embed bad habits?

♦ Do you use retrieval practice strategies to support students working from memory?

♦ Do you make the links between topics explicit to students?

♦ Do you find opportunities to link topics from last week, last month and last term?

♦ Do you provide the students with lots of opportunities to practise answering exam questions?

♦ Do you use scaffolds appropriately to support students?

♦ Do you use knowledge organisers to make the key knowledge explicit to students?

Chapter 5

Questioning

Let's start by thinking about the purpose of questioning. Why do we, as PE teachers, need to ask questions to our students? This question can cause quite a stir. Kathleen Cotton offers an insightful perspective, as she suggests there are five main reasons for asking questions:[1]

1   To test understanding of a new concept.

   ♦ *What are the three main teaching points of the lay-up in basketball?*

2   To deepen and develop understanding.

   ♦ *Why is width an effective principle of attack in football?*

3   To ensure students take a share in the cognitive work of the classroom.

---

1   Kathleen Cotton, Classroom Questioning. Close-Up Number 5. *School Improvement Research Series III* (Portland, OR: Northwest Regional Educational Lab, 1989). Available at: https://educationnorthwest.org/sites/default/files/ClassroomQuestioning.pdf.

♦ *What is the first thing to think about when starting a gymnastics floor routine?*

4 To help you form and sustain your classroom culture.

♦ *What are we going to do when we get back to our courts? [Getting a student to repeat instructions back to you if you suspect they weren't listening to you.]*

5 To create curiosity.

♦ *How could we develop the motif to show a change in dynamics?*

In PE, the first two are our most common purposes. We tend to ask more factual recall-based questions to check understanding, potentially about key teaching points or when checking that students understand the parameters of the practice. Open questions are used to deepen or develop knowledge. Kathleen distinguishes between lower and higher cognitive questions. Lower cognitive questions are more commonly framed around recall, whereas higher cognitive questions will usually probe students' ability to use that knowledge and apply it to a specific context or evaluate it in a succinct way. For example, on the topic of technology in GCSE PE theory, a lower cognitive question might be:

Which technological development in football supports officials in their decision making?

A higher cognitive question on the same topic might be:

In football, how effective has video assistant referee (VAR) technology been over the last season? Explain and justify your answer.

There isn't a hierarchy here, and we shouldn't be aiming to only ask higher cognitive questions. Our choice of question comes back to the purpose of our questioning. Lower cognitive questions are useful for improving recall or committing new knowledge to memory. It could be said that good recall-based questioning supports the key principle of retrieval practice. Higher cognitive questions are purposeful when trying to deepen understanding, link topics or apply knowledge. The fundamental takeaway is that the question needs to elicit the correct response in order to avoid any misconceptions being embedded. It also needs to make the students think.

Dylan Wiliam and Paul Black unpick what makes a good question.[2] They suggest the following as characteristics of a good question:

- Promotes discussion.

- Everyone should be able to have a go at it.

- Makes students think.

- Has a specific purpose.

We have already touched on the final characteristic: purpose. The other three points provide an interesting opportunity to reflect, leading us to think about our own practice in both the classroom and teaching space. Do we ensure that our questions involve the whole class, elicit thinking, promote discussion and are accessible to all? If this is the gold standard when it comes to questioning, it is certainly worth thinking about. We will explore eliciting thinking and discussion further as we move through this chapter.

Questioning is a vital part of good PE teaching; it is the most efficient way of gathering information from students about their current level of knowledge. This information can then be used to shape the lesson moving forward. It is undeniable that questioning is a crucial part of PE teaching.

---

2 Dylan William and Paul Black, *Inside the Black Box: Raising Standards Through Classroom Assessment* (London: GL Assessment, 1990).

Before we explore some questioning strategies, it is useful to discuss the mistakes that teachers often make:

♦ **Wait time.** Our questions should elicit thinking, so we need to ensure that we provide students with enough time to think before responding. Too often, the time given to students is insufficient, usually less than a second. To overcome this, we can use strategies like Dylan Wiliam's Pause-Pose-Pounce-Bounce[3] (where the teacher poses a question, pauses for 3–5 seconds and then pounces on a student to give a response followed by bouncing another question to another student around the room), or ask students a question and let them know you are coming back to them for the answer in three minutes' time.

♦ **Subject knowledge.** Our responses following students' answers can sometimes lack clarity or depth. As with much of this book, our ability to be high-quality educators stands or falls on our subject knowledge. We need to be able to engage with the multitude of responses that the students could give and be very aware of how our words could be (mis)interpreted to avoid embedding misconceptions.

♦ **Few students involved.** Questioning can sometimes involve only a few students, usually the ones we know are going to give a good response. We need to develop strategies to ensure that all students are involved in the questions we pose. Being explicit about think time can alleviate this. Ask the question, insist on silence and give students 30 seconds of no talking to encourage them to think of a response. This can then be followed by a discussion in pairs or by picking several students to give you their responses.

♦ **Accepting poor responses.** Due to time constraints or our slightly misguided view that it will make students feel

---

3   See Tom Sherrington and Sara Stafford, Questioning Techniques: 7. Pause-Pose-Pounce-Bounce (Chartered College of Teaching, 2018). Available at: https://my.chartered.college/wp-content/uploads/2018/10/7.-Pose-Pause-Pounce-Bounce-1.pdf.

better about themselves, we often accept poor responses from students, and supply or embellish the answers ourselves. We need to make sure that we address incorrect answers, while ensuring that the students feel confident enough to respond to future questions. This boils down to the culture in our classrooms and lessons.

♦ **Ineffective questions.** Asking questions that provide very little challenge, usually about something that has been said by the teacher only a few minutes beforehand. Unsurprisingly, the vast majority of students will be able to recall the answer, but they will be unlikely to do so in a few lessons' time. This comes back to ensuring that questions elicit thinking.

♦ **'I don't know' responses.** Too often, teachers move on to other students using strategies like 'phone a friend', without scaffolding their questioning or attempting to build the student's response following 'I don't know'. Later in this chapter, we will explore the use of rephrasing, multiple-choice questions, reminding students of the facts or providing an answer and asking the students to explain the why.

♦ **Ping-pong.** If the questions are only directed back and forth between the teacher and one student, it can be tedious for the rest of the class. They may as well be thinking about what they are going to have for lunch. Dylan Wiliam suggests that a lesson should not be like table tennis with the questions rallied between a teacher and one student. Instead, it is like a basketball game: the ball is transferred around the whole team and the teacher is the point guard, bringing others into play.[4]

♦ **Questioning too early.** We sometimes question students when they don't really have the knowledge to answer because they haven't been taught it yet. It can sometimes feel like a game of 'Guess what's in the teacher's head'. We simply need to explain the new knowledge to them

---

4 Wiliam, *Embedded Formative Assessment.*

prior to any questions. After all, we are the expert in the room.

Questioning Strategies

1. Dialogic Questioning

Dialogic questioning is where the teacher asks an initial question and then follows up with a range of questions based on the student's response. The aim is to probe and deepen students' thinking. Dialogic questioning provides more clarity for the teacher regarding the level of understanding. The art of this type of questioning is in engaging the whole class. This can be done by bouncing questions around the room, each building on the previous response. When it is most effective, it seems like a conversation that's delving deeper and deeper into the topic. As with any good questioning strategy, strong subject knowledge is non-negotiable. You will also need to know where you want the students to go, so your questioning can guide them and their thinking in the correct direction. For example, when teaching the set shot in volleyball, the questioning may run as follows:

Teacher: What are three things to remember when playing the set shot [*pause to allow thinking time*] … Sienna?

Sienna: Wide high elbows; whole body push through the ball; use your fingertips, not your palms.

Teacher: Yes. Why do you need to use your fingertips, not your palms … Charlie?

Charlie: So you have more control over the ball.

Teacher: What will that control enable you to do … Mark?

Mark: Get the ball to a teammate who may then be able to play a spike.

Teacher: Excellent. When would you use the set shot then … Reggie?

Reggie: After a serve.

Teacher: Well, yes, but what is the determining factor … Ellie?

Ellie: When you can get to the ball and it is still above your head.

Teacher: Correct. What would you do if the ball was below your head … Clissy?

Clissy: Play the dig.

Teacher: What would the following shot be after the dig … Ollie?

Ollie: A set.

Teacher: With what aim?

This process could go on and on. Through relentless and well-thought-out questioning, the teacher is teasing out all of the key points but also really delving into the students' understanding of the wider game. As with most questioning strategies, there is a lot of crossover and good questioning will link several strategies together. For example, the teacher in this instance encouraged thinking and active participation by pausing and allowing time for the students to think, coupled with cold calling to support all students being engaged. Even if they are not called upon to verbalise their answer, they know that they could be, so they will need to do the thinking.

2. Metacognitive Questioning

Metacognition is a somewhat slippery concept. In simple terms, it is about the way in which we get students to plan, monitor and evaluate their learning. If we are going to get metacognition right, it is fundamentally about changing students' behaviour. If we are going to make this change, we need to first address how we, as the teacher, provide the students with opportunities to develop their metacognition and self-regulation. We have already touched on metacognitive modelling; in this chapter, we are going to look at how we can question the students metacognitively. The aim here is to support students in becoming more self-regulatory. The EEF suggests that metacognition and self-regulation are domain specific.[5] Chris Runeckles, director of the Durrington Research School, offers some metacognitive questions linked to planning, monitoring and evaluating. PE teachers can use these when questioning students (see page 109).

Please see an example of metacognitive questioning when looking at defending in Year 9 handball:

- What is the purpose of defending?

- What is the first thing to do when your team loses possession? Why is that so important?

- Why did I ask you that question?

- Why is the 5:1 defence strategy (five zonal defenders round the D and one wasp who chases the ball until the opposing team get the ball to near the D) effective?

- What is the most difficult bit of defending?

- What are the principles of defending?

- Why are you effective when defending as a team in this way?

- What aspects did you struggle with in your defensive strategy?

- What can you do to try to regain possession?

- In what other situations would this defensive strategy be useful? Why do you think that?

---

5   Perry et al., *Cognitive Science Approaches in the Classroom.*

Knowledge of task	Knowledge of self	Knowledge of strategies
Is the task too challenging for me? What are the most difficult aspects of this task? How much time should I devote to this task? Are there any easy bits I can get done?	Is this task asking for subject knowledge that I can remember? Do I understand the concepts that underpin this task? Am I motivated to stick at this tricky task? What can I do to keep myself focused?	Are my notes effective for understanding this task? Do I need to ask for help? What strategies can I deploy if I am stuck? What can I do to ensure that I remember what I've learnt?

- If your team were conceding too many goals, what could you do differently?

- What is the most difficult part of the 5:1 strategy?

- How are you going to transition from attack to defence next time you play handball?

3. Participation Ratio

Too often, teachers pose a really thought-provoking question, an enthusiastic student raises their hand and offers a response with some partially correct information, the teacher then cleverly fills in the gaps. Brilliant! Everyone in the class now knows the answer. If only this was the case. A more realistic reflection might be that when the question was posed, some students were thinking about what they are going to do at the weekend, some were distracting their friends with silly facial expressions and some were thinking, 'Please don't pick me; I have no idea.' The one student who offered a response and gave the partially accurate answer will still hold those misconceptions despite the teacher correcting them in their reply. It seems the rest of the class weren't listening sufficiently to the original question, let alone the response. What we need to do is increase the participation ratio in the class; ideally, we want all students to think deeply about the question we pose. The question is: how?

In practical lessons, this can be done through Frank Lyman's think, pair, share.[6] This is where the teacher poses a question, then pauses for 10–12 seconds. During this time, the teacher would be seen looking at the students. This is more a superficial look so the students feel that need to think as they may be asked to share their ideas with you and the class. After this thinking time, the teacher gets the students to share their response with a partner. The teacher can predetermine the pairs and who will be talking first. The pairs discuss their thinking and then the teacher calls on them to share their answers with the group. At this point, the teacher facilitates a whole-class discussion, which can involve dialogic and metacognitive questions. There are some traps to avoid when using this strategy. Ensure you are explicit with the thinking time and approach any students who appear obviously off-task with non-invasive strategies like raising an eyebrow, holding eye contact or tapping the table to regain focus. Assign specific roles for the paired talking (e.g. 'Partner A, you have 10 seconds to share your idea [*pause*]. Now, partner B, you have 10 seconds to share your thoughts.').

In theory lessons, and in practical where appropriate, mini whiteboards provide no opt out for students. Adam Boxer suggests that they can be used for students to write down their response, rather than verbalise their answers.[7] In this way, the teacher can quickly see whether everyone has supplied a response. They can circulate the class, providing students with prompts or stretching their thinking. The teacher can also use this as a formative assessment strategy

---

6   Frank Lyman, The Responsive Classroom Discussion. In A. S. Anderson (ed.), *Mainstreaming Digest* (College Park, MD: University of Maryland College of Education, 1981), pp. 109–113.

7   Adam Boxer, To Make Sure Your Students are Ready to Practise, Use Mini Whiteboards [video]. *Tips for Teachers* (10 March 2022). Available at: https://www.youtube.com/watch?v=9OxEZRQu3NI.

to support their planning of the next task or the wider curriculum. When discussing answers, the teacher can call on individual students to share their answers verbally or ask the whole class to hold up their whiteboards in unison. This ensures that students are thinking about the question and gives them time to prepare well-thought-out answers. Metacognitive and/or dialogic questions can then follow.

4. Delayed Response

When we are using our lower cognitive questions to check what a student knows, quick-fire questions and answers will suffice. If we are asking a higher cognitive question to check how deeply a student understands a concept or how effectively they can apply their knowledge in an unfamiliar context, we need to provide them with sufficient time to think and prepare their response. A good way to do this is to let students know in advance that you are going to ask them a question, explain the question and let them know how long they have before you require their response. An added positive to this method is that it takes away some of the angst around answering as it gives them sufficient time to consider a response.

This strategy is equally effective in both practical and theory lessons. For example, in a theory lesson, when students are completing a task on performance-enhancing drugs and their impact, you could pose a question along the lines of: 'Can anyone name one advantage or disadvantage of taking a stimulant? In three minutes' time, I'm going to choose someone to answer.' Similarly, at the start of a practical lesson, you could pose a question that you want them to be able to answer at the end of the lesson. For example, in handball when looking at defending as a unit, tell them at the start: 'At the end of today's lesson I want you to tell me what you think the best defensive strategy is and explain why you think it's the most effective.' This will encourage the students to be thinking throughout the lesson.

5. Cold Calling

Doug Lemov came up with the idea of cold calling, which is a very simple yet highly effective strategy.[8] Often, we see questions like 'Tom, can you tell me a component of fitness needed in the 100m?' In your class of 32, 31 students not called Tom switched off from what you were saying as soon as you said 'Tom'. They are safe in the knowledge that they are not going to be asked that question. It is much better to reshape the questions and subtly tweak the order to: 'What component of fitness do you need at the start of the 100m *[pause]*, Tom?' The question asks the same thing but there are now 32 students thinking of the answer, as they may be asked to share their response. From the one question, you are generating thought across the whole class. The pause is to allow sufficient wait time. The idea of posing a question, pausing for a period of time and then pouncing with a student's name requires very little planning but can have a huge impact on the participation ratio.

---

8   Lemov, *Teach Like a Champion.*

6. Elaborative Questioning

Elaborative questioning is a really effective strategy for PE teachers to use to find out whether students deeply understand a topic or concept. Simply put, elaborative questioning asks what, how, who, when, where and why. The information gained will enable the teacher to decide whether they are confident that the students know this topic or there are still some misconceptions that need to be unpicked. For example, in a handball lesson the teacher may go through these elaborative questions:

♦ What is the name of the position who plays as the 1 in the 5:1 defence system?

♦ When would the wasp transition into attack?

♦ How would they decide when they need to press the opposition players?

♦ Where on the court would they start to press?

♦ Who would be best suited to this position? What attributes do they need?

♦ Why is the wasp a crucial position to get right?

This would be an equally effective strategy in theory lessons. For example, when teaching spirometry, the teacher may go through these elaborative questions:

- What is the definition of tidal volume?

- How does exercise affect tidal volume?

- When would tidal volume increase but be a constant depth?

- What would happen to inspiratory reserve volume (IRV) and expiratory reserve volume (ERV) if tidal volume were to increase?

- Who would need their tidal volume to increase gradually?

- Why does residual volume always stay the same regardless of tidal volume?

Bouncing questions round the room, using mini whiteboards or deploying the think, pair, share strategy can work with elaborative questioning. It does take time to plan, but the information you gain from the responses can be used to shape what you do next.

7. What to Do About 'I Don't Know'

When we ask students a question, they are likely to give one of these five responses:

1   An accurate and detailed answer.

2   An accurate but underdeveloped answer.

3   A partially accurate answer, with a bit of tangential waffle.

4   A completely inaccurate or irrelevant answer.

5   An 'I don't know' or a shrug of the shoulders.

The gold standard here is number 1. Numbers 2–4 are important and need to be addressed so as to ensure that misconceptions do not become embedded. However, number 5 is by far the trickiest to deal with, as this feeds directly into the culture of your classroom or teaching space. We need to ensure we scaffold accordingly so that all students know that this will not be tolerated in your lessons. Rather than accepting 'I don't know' or asking peers to help out, we need to reshape or rephrase the question to enable the student to answer. Muijs and Reynolds suggest that the effect of achievement on self-concept is stronger than the effect of self-concept on achievement.[9] Therefore, if we want to motivate our students by helping them to see themselves as successful, they need to be answering questions confidently and correctly. Some of the ways to tackle 'I don't know' are:

♦ **Rephrase the question.** The onus should be on the question being worded poorly, not the student's inability to answer it.

---

9 Daniel Muijs and David Reynolds, *Effective Teaching: Evidence and Practice*, 4th edn (London Sage, 2018), p. 163.

Teacher: Why is it really important that we know how to serve correctly in table tennis?

Student: I don't know.

Teacher: Sorry, I've not worded that question very well. When do you serve in table tennis?

Student: To start the point.

Teacher: And what happens if you can't serve correctly?

Student: If you can't serve, you won't ever be able to win a point.

♦ **Turn it into multiple choice.** The distractors need to be plausible.

Teacher: What is a transition?

Student: I don't know.

Teacher: Is it movement between balances, a change in height of the balances, or ensuring you hold your balance for 3 seconds?

Student: Movement between balances.

♦ **Let them tell you why the answer is correct.** Give them the answer, but ask them to explain it.

Teacher: Why would a sprinter need to have protein after a weight training session?

Student: I don't know.

Teacher: OK, well when you weight train, your muscles develop microtears. Protein allows the muscles to repair more quickly, meaning you will be able to train again sooner. Protein in the diet is for growth and repair of the muscle tissue. Why would a sprinter need to have more protein than a marathon runner?

Student: Because they need to have more muscle mass due to needing more strength and power.

♦ **Remind them of what they do know.** Offer prompts and build on existing knowledge.

Teacher: What is the most important component of fitness in the marathon?

Student: I don't know.

Teacher: Well, what components of fitness do we need in the marathon?

Student: Reaction time, muscular endurance, cardiovascular endurance, agility, speed.

Teacher: Brilliant. If we need reaction time at the start, agility to react to unexpected hazards, and speed at the end, which components will we need throughout the whole race?

Student: Cardiovascular endurance and muscular endurance.

There may be a multitude of reasons why a student responds with 'I don't know', from general defiance to panic, cognitive overload to a lack of knowledge. You will need to use your professional judgement – as the expert on the children you teach – to tailor your response. The one thing you certainly don't want to do is make the students more reluctant to answer questions in the future. Therefore, avoid phrases like 'You should know this' or 'We only did this last lesson', and avoid repeating the question without modification.

Reflective Questions

- Do you have a clear vision of how you want questioning to run in your lessons?

- How do you deal with 'I don't know' responses?

- Do you use a combination of lower and higher cognitive questions?

- Do you insist on students elaborating on their initial answers?

- Do you question the majority of students in the majority of your lessons?

- Do you ask metacognitive questions?

- Do you give students sufficient thinking time to consider and formulate their responses?

- How do you foster a culture in which students are confident enough to ask and answer questions?

- How do you ensure that all students think about responses to your questions?

Chapter 6

Feedback

There is a wealth of research evidence looking into feedback and the impact it can have, if timely, on learning. The EEF Teaching and Learning Toolkit ranks feedback as the number one strand in terms of effect on learning.[1] The most important thing when it comes to feedback, as Dylan Wiliam suggests, 'is what students do with it.'[2]

As PE teachers, we should be using a variety of feedback strategies for a number of different purposes. Ultimately, feedback has four main roles: to show students what they need to aim for, to keep them on the right path, to let them know whether they have got there or not, and to point them in the direction of the next step or target. The key component of any type of feedback is that it is a two-way process. It should not be seen as something the teacher simply delivers to the student. It is a process in which the teacher and

---

1   See: https://educationendowmentfoundation.org.uk/education-evidence/
     teaching-learning-toolkit.

2   Dylan Wiliam, The Secret of Effective Feedback, *Educational Leadership*, 73(7)
     (2016). Available at: https://www.ascd.org/el/articles/the-secret-of-effective-
     feedback.

the student pass information back and forth between each other, as seen in the following diagram:

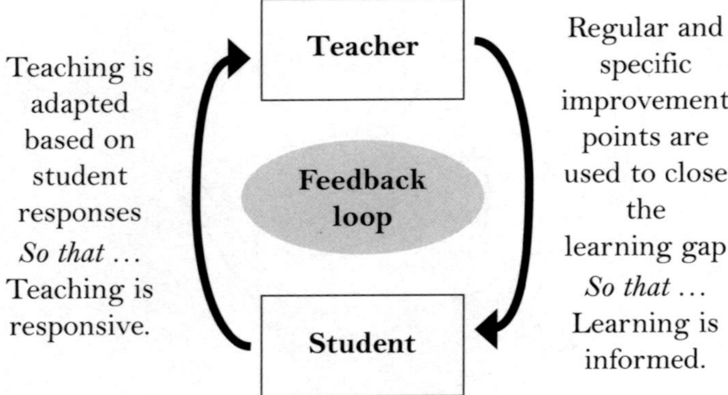

Teaching is adapted based on student responses *So that …* Teaching is responsive.

Regular and specific improvement points are used to close the learning gap *So that …* Learning is informed.

As teachers, we identify the 'learning gap' – the space between where they are now in their knowledge and skills and where we want them to be – and then provide feedback aimed at closing that gap. The feedback we get from the students helps us to know exactly how to close that gap and enables us to plan what to do next. We should always use the feedback we get from students about how they are performing in our lessons to inform our future planning. One thought to keep at the forefront of our minds is articulated succinctly by Dylan Wiliam: 'Feedback should be more work for the recipient than the donor.'[3]

The feedback strategies we use should fit these principles:

♦ Feedback that simply tells students what to do is unhelpful – *when doing high jump, drive up with your inside knee.* This type of feedback compounds dependency.

---

3   Dylan Wiliam, The Formative Evaluation of Teaching Performance. Centre for Strategic Education Occasional Paper 137 (September 2014), p. 15. Available at: https://www.dylanwiliam.org/Dylan_Wiliams_website/Publications_files/The%20formative%20evaluation%20of%20teaching%20performance%20%28CSE%202014%29%20secure.pdf. See also, Wiliam, *Embedded Formative Assessment.*

- Feedback should make students think about their work and how they could improve it – *what do you need to do to ensure your lead leg doesn't clip the bar on your way up?* This type of feedback develops autonomy.

- Feedback should make students do something to improve. If it doesn't achieve this, then it is a waste of time – *now you have identified that the lead leg is too close to the bar, re-mark your run up, practise the take-off element and correct your distances.*

- Feedback should keep students in the struggle zone. If it allows them to languish in the comfort zone, or pushes them into the panic zone, then learning will be limited.

- Feedback should be manageable and sustainable for teachers. This is key for teacher workload and well-being.

Feedback Strategies

1. Self-Checking

In both practical and theory PE, there are some things that are either correct or incorrect (e.g. labelling the cardiac cycle, serving in badminton, definitions of the components of fitness, a lay-up in basketball). In theory lessons, the most efficient way to give students feedback is to go through the answers with them, asking them to check their work as you go. Students should get into the habit of amending their mistakes as you work through the answers. In practical lessons, this is usually down to the outcome of the skill. The feedback should be on the teaching points so students can self-check which teaching point they aren't getting right, therefore impacting the success of the skill. In both practical and theory lessons, the teacher can scan the room and see how the students are getting on. From this, you can see if there are any common misconceptions or mistakes that the students have made, reteaching the topic or providing whole-class feedback if required.

Following retrieval practice quizzes, you can get more detailed feedback on how the class has done by simply asking them how many out of ten they got correct. The point here is that we don't just want to know how many a student got right, we want to be able to know where students struggled, what students do and don't know. This can be developed further by asking for hands up for a correct response after each question. This can be useful as it gives feedback to the teacher on whether there is one particular topic or question that a lot of students are struggling with in terms of recall or understanding. This may require immediate intervention from the teacher.

This approach is an effective form of feedback as it gives both the teacher and the students instant feedback on performance (as individuals and as a whole class), requires students to address their mistakes and, most importantly, is manageable and sustainable for the teacher.

2. Live Marking

Live marking is a highly effective strategy in both practical and theory PE. We want to give students feedback about their understanding of a specific concept or skill there and then. This will also limit the chances of misconceptions becoming embedded. While students are answering questions, look in their books, focusing on the current key learning for that lesson. Pose a question verbally or write one in their book to correct a misunderstanding or develop their thinking further. In practical lessons, you can observe their performance of a task and ask questions to help focus their practice on areas for improvement. Ask them to respond, allow them time to think about it and move away. Come back in a few minutes to check that they have responded. This is a useful feedback strategy as it requires immediate action from the student. An example from a Year 10 lesson follows:

Using your knowledge of muscles and bone explain how they work together to produce movement. give an example (5 marks)

- muscles pull the bone via the tendon
- as the biceps contract the triceps relax at flexion at the elbow
- the articulating bones are the ulna and radius
- The tendons are at the shoulder and elbow to assit movement (muscle to bone)
- flexion at the elbow is a hinge joint

What is the contracting muscle called?
the agonist - e.g. biceps.
What is the relaxing muscle called?
the antagonist - e.g. triceps
What does articulating bones mean?
the bones that move - when the elbow flexes.
Point of origin is at the Humerus
Point of insertion is at the radius

Obviously, it is unrealistic to think that you will be able to do this for every student in every lesson. However, once you get into the habit of doing this while circling the classroom, over the course of a week or a unit of work you will be able to get around every student. Alternatively, you could target your efforts, focusing on specific students who may have been underachieving or who you know have a particular gap in knowledge.

3. Checklists

All too often, PE teachers use non-doers (students who are injured or otherwise unable to take part in the practical lesson) as coaches or to provide feedback for a partner.

Understanding assessment criteria or identifying areas of weakness in a practical performance requires expert subject knowledge. Understanding and articulating the specifics about how to improve is hard for some adults. Therefore, it could be suggested that students may struggle to provide accurate, detailed and correct feedback. There is a very real risk that by misinterpreting the criteria, students will give incorrect feedback to either their peers or themselves and embed misconceptions.

A way to try to alleviate this is through the use of checklists. If they are concise and specific, they can be given to students while they are tackling a problem to help them ensure that they are responding appropriately. The problem can be either a theoretical concept or task in a theory lesson or developing a skill in a practical lesson. The checklist will provide students with an evaluative resource which they can use while completing their work. This type of self-reflection can also support their metacognitive development.

For example, students often struggle with answering 9-mark questions. So, rather than waiting for them to make the mistakes and having to provide individual feedback, why not provide students with a checklist form to use, like the one that follows?

Step	Action	Completed?
1	Box the command word, circle the marks, identify the correct structure of the response.	
2	Underline the key words and the sport. Define the key words.	

Step	Action	Completed?
3	Apply the key words to the relevant sport.	
4	Give five AO3 sentences, leading to a well-rounded conclusive comment.	

Checklists are also useful in practical lessons too. For example, students will often get overwhelmed by the number of rules when serving in table tennis. What follows is an example of a checklist that students can use:

Rule	Tick when secure
Ball in an open palm.	
Held above the height of the table.	
Ball raised 6 inches off of the hand.	
Contact behind the line of the table.	
Ball bounced on both sides of the table.	
Variation of serve, imparting pressure on your opponent.	

The statements need to be short, concise and easy for students to understand and check their work against. If there is any room for misinterpretation or deliberation over whether they have or have not met the criteria, then they cease to be helpful. Done well, they are useful as they instil a sense of confidence by showing students how to break down a complex problem. As with any scaffold, you do not want students to become overreliant on it. However, in the early stages of practice, checklists can support with managing cognitive load while trying to move students from dependency to independence.

4. Mini Whiteboards

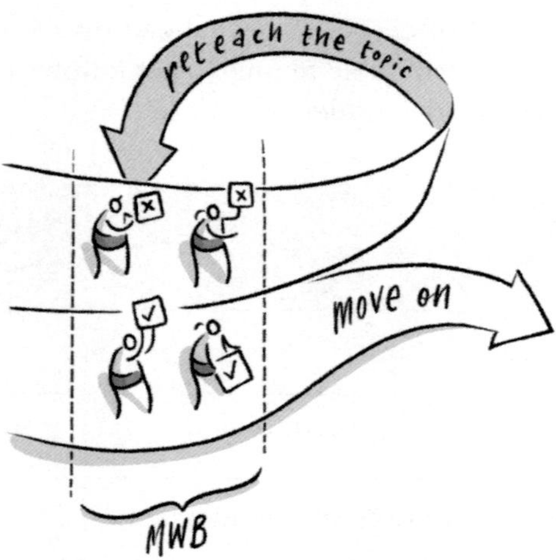

We have already touched on mini whiteboards in Chapter 5. They are useful in providing the teacher with immediate feedback about how well a class has understood a specific concept or idea. In terms of feedback, the points to consider regarding their effective use are:

♦ **Set the culture.** This is about you finding out what students do and do not know. There is no pressure on them to get the answers correct; it is about you finding out information that you can use to shape future tasks and lessons.

- **Allow enough thinking time.** Ask the question, insist on silence and do not allow them to check back in their books. Count down to students holding up their whiteboards so they all show their answer at the same time.

- **Follow up with more questions.** Interrogate students on their responses (e.g. why did you pick that? How did you get to that answer? Where do you think you went wrong? Can you expand on that response?). Once this becomes a mainstay in your lessons, students will know what is coming and they will start to think more deeply about their responses.

- **Respond when appropriate.** If a number of students get the answer wrong, use this information and reteach the topic.

- **Procedural knowledge is equally important.** Mini whiteboards are best used to check objective facts using questions that have right or wrong answers. However, they can be used to check procedural knowledge, which goes hand in hand with declarative knowledge. For example, when modelling the box, circle, underline method (see Chapter 3), the teacher could ask, 'What is the first thing I do with this question?' The teacher can then check whether all students understand the first stage of the process. They would use this information to question further, proceed with the next stage or, if a number of students were incorrect in their response, reteach the strategy.

- **Support retrieval practice.** Questions can be in the same format as the quiz structure explained in Chapter 4, including questions about content covered in the last lesson, last week and last term.

For example, when teaching the 100m sprint in Key Stage 3 athletics, mini whiteboards could be used at the start of lesson to find out what students already know regarding phases of the race and the components of fitness involved. An opening question could be 'What are the three most important components of fitness in the 100m?' Allow one minute for students to write down their thoughts independently. Then verbally unpick students' answers and their reasons why, giving students an opportunity to agree, build on or challenge each other's thoughts through targeted questioning. Address any misconceptions or incorrect answers. Then use the mini whiteboards again to build on this knowledge and link components of fitness to different sporting situations, to cement the students' wider understanding of their application of the components of fitness. This could be done through further questioning.

5. Whole-Class Feedback

When I think back to my NQT year, I would spend a lot of time walking around the room giving students feedback on individual mistakes that they were making. If I had paused and taken a step back, I would have noticed that the mistakes could have been rectified by stopping the task and giving some whole-class feedback. Another benefit to whole-class feedback, besides the obvious time it saves you, is the control it gives you over the interpretation of your feedback. As Dylan Wiliam suggests, the most important thing about feedback is what students do with it. If you offer 32 different pieces of feedback, it is very difficult to control the interpretation or what is done with it. However, whole-class feedback allows you more control over how it is understood and interpreted and, perhaps most importantly, what is done with it by tweaking a drill to sharpen the focus of the students' practice linked to the feedback you have just given. This is the case in both theory and practical lessons, as outlined in Chapter 1.

Harry Fletcher-Wood proposes the following system when thinking about whole-class feedback.[4] Although his background is a history one, there are some principles that directly link to PE.

♦ Reteach – using fresh examples.

♦ Revisit goals – clarify goals with models and checklists.

♦ Revise the process – model the process live or with worked examples.

♦ Redraft, practise and check – allow students to stay in the struggle zone through further practice.

This provides a good framework for how to approach whole-class feedback. Strategies for implementing this framework in both theory and practical PE include:

♦ **Start again.** Sometimes you will look through a few books or observe students performing a task and they simply don't get it or can't do it. Rather than carrying on uphill, sun in your eyes and into a headwind, stop and start that topic or task again with some slight modifications so the students can understand and complete the task or practical activity. For example, if you are trying to teach the 3-set play in volleyball but students are struggling with playing an effective dig to set up the play, don't carry on. Pause that activity and go back over how

---

4   Harry Fletcher-Wood, Guiding Student Improvement Without Individual Feedback, *Improving Teaching* [blog] (18 June 2017). Available at: https:// improvingteaching.co.uk/2017/06/18/guiding-student-improvement-without-individual-feedback/.

to perform an effective dig, followed by some purposeful practice.

♦ **Pick out common themes.** Following a mock GCSE exam or a full-context practical activity, it is far more purposeful to give whole-class as opposed to individual feedback. When marking the mocks, note down common misconceptions that come up, rather than providing individual feedback. Your feedback lesson could involve reteaching the common misconceptions to the whole class. In a practical lesson, this could be done when observing the full-context game, with your feedback on common mistakes used to shape the start of the next lesson. For example, if you notice a lot of students are diving in when playing a small-sided game of football, then the following lesson could cover one-on-one defending.

♦ **Remodel it.** In theory lessons, you can live model your own answer to a question, including narrating the implicit processes you go through as the expert. Highlight each step where students tend to make mistakes and explain how to overcome them. In practical lessons, this doesn't change. If you notice that students are making similar mistakes, then remodel the skills, highlighting where they are getting it wrong. Include the *what* as well as the *how* in your remodel. For example, if you notice several students are performing a lay-up with an under-arm release with limited success, remodel the overarm release, explaining why it is more effective or questioning the students. With an overhead lay-up, you can get the ball closer to the backboard, limiting the things that can go wrong.

♦ **Break down a worked example.** In theory lessons, choose an example of a successful student response to an exam question. Copy it and get students to stick it in their books. Divide the next page into two columns. In one column, write down all the features of the answer that are strong and correct; in the other, list the areas for improvement. You will need to model how to do this a few times before expecting students to do it effectively and independently. In practical lessons, the principle doesn't change. Use a video clip or model a skill several times and ask students to think about what is strong about the performance and what needs improving. Student responses can be verbalised or summarised on the whiteboard for everyone to refer back to during practice.

♦ **Emergency stop.** Sometimes you will notice that students are getting something which is fundamental to the successful completion of the task or activity totally wrong. It is absolutely fine to stop and reteach, remodel or address the problem there and then.

6. Verbal Feedback

In practical lessons, we will use verbal feedback more often than any other form – the power of verbal feedback should not be underestimated. Simply put, verbal feedback consists of the teacher – the expert in the room (or on the pitch) – telling the student how to get better. This could be for a number of purposes:

♦ To fine-tune specific practical skills in a range of sporting activities.

♦ To deepen their thinking around decision making and applying their skills to wider contexts.

♦ To reflect upon and improve their performance and decision making.

♦ To improve their written work, including responses to exam questions.

♦ To apply their knowledge to a range of different contexts in theory lessons.

As previously mentioned, the power of feedback lies in what students do with it. Therefore, following verbal feedback, it is important to check students' understanding of what they have been told and how they are going to use it to change something in their work. Following verbal feedback, we should always aim to return to a student after a few minutes to check whether they have made the required improvements.

Delivering verbal feedback is like bowling. What piece of information can you, the teacher, provide to the student that is going to hit the head pin and knock all of the others down? What will have the biggest impact on the students' development of the specific skill, technique or tactical understanding? Check that the student understands the feedback and why it is important and that they have time to act on it through purposeful practice. When verbal feedback is done poorly, it is either irreplicable for the student – they can't recall and repeat it – or it focuses on something that is not going to develop their performance or understanding.

7. Formative Use of Summative Assessment

When we give students a marked mock exam back, all too often they pay no attention to anything other than the score and the grade. In order to support students in looking more at the process than the outcome, we need to flip the narrative and change student behaviour. We want them to look at what they did well, what they didn't do so well, where they dropped marks and why, and think about what they are going to do to ensure they do not make the same mistakes next time. This starts with our formative use of summative assessments, rather than revealing scores and grades, looking at where students fell down in the mock and why this was the case. Was it due to subject knowledge and grasp of the content? Was it the wording of the question, the structure of their response, or something else? We need to provide students with the opportunity to unpick what they struggled with and the reasons why. Our feedback should be shaped around the *what* and the *why*, leading students to grapple with the *how* of improving. We can factor this into our feedback and future planning, while supporting students in their metacognitive development. This information can be taken in through one-on-one learning conversations, group discussion or learning reflection sheets, an example of which follows:

1. Are you **happy** with your PE mock result? Explain why.	
2. Did you perform **better** in Paper 1 or Paper 2?	
3. What was your **strongest** topic in Paper 1?	
4. What was your **weakest** topic in Paper 1?	
5. What was your **strongest** topic in Paper 2?	
6. What was your **weakest** topic in Paper 2?	
7. What were the **two hardest questions** to answer in Paper 1? Explain why.	Q __ Q __
8. What were the **two hardest questions** to answer in Paper 2? Explain why.	Q __ Q __
9. How many **hours of revision**, including Period 7, did you complete in preparation for your PE mock exams?	

10. What **revision techniques and/or approaches** did you use to prepare for your PE mock exams? Do you feel they were effective?	
11. **Rank** the following aspects of your PE learning from most urgent to improve (1) to least urgent to improve (3): *Subject knowledge, time management, understanding the question.*	1 2 3
12. From today, will your preparations for the real GCSE PE exams in the summer term change? If so, how? If not, why not?	

Reflective Questions

- Do you ensure that students respond to the feedback that you give them?

- Does your feedback help to inform your planning?

- Are students given sufficient time and guidance to interpret and use your feedback?

- Are your feedback techniques manageable and sustainable?

- How do you ensure that the feedback you give is actioned by students?

- Do you use formative assessment strategies to support your targeted feedback?

Final Thoughts

The six principles that have been discussed in this book are underpinned by evidence from educational specialists and findings from cognitive science. However, it has also been very heavily informed by some excellent PE teachers whom I have had the privilege of working with over the past 12 years.

All of these teachers have several things in common. They have the highest of expectations of what the students they teach can achieve, regardless of their starting points. They challenge students to be the best versions of themselves. They are highly skilled at explaining the complexities inherent within the wide range of sporting activities they teach. Modelling is an integral part of their practice, affording students very deliberate and purposeful opportunities to practise newly acquired knowledge and skills, punctuated with timely and specific questioning and feedback.

Central to their expert teaching is their dedication to ensuring that their subject knowledge is impeccable. This – coupled with their ability to build strong, positive and professional relationships with their students – enables them to be exceptional PE teachers. These building blocks are non-negotiable and allow them to implement the pedagogical principles discussed in this book effectively. They do this by:

♦ Expecting excellence from every student they come across, in absolutely everything that they do – their effort, their work, their behaviour, their attendance, their punctuality, their manners, everything. This includes lesson time, social time, extracurricular clubs, in between lessons – everywhere.

♦ Getting to know the students and taking a genuine interest in them as people, knowing what they like or dislike, what they can do, what they struggle with, when they need to be pushed and when they need to be supported.

♦ Engaging, enthusing and supporting students. They build bridges and connect with even the hardest to reach students, finding out something about them and showing an interest in how they are doing in and out of school. They consistently demonstrate a real passion for the subject of PE, showing all students how amazing the subject is.

♦ Being honest, believing in their students, never giving up on them and finding their successes. They help students to build resilience even in the tough times, celebrate student successes, push students to maximise their efforts, hold them to account and believe they can – with hard work and dedication – achieve amazing things.

♦ Knowing the subject of PE inside out. Not only does this mean they teach it really well, but it also instils students' confidence in their ability to teach superbly. Students want to feel safe and secure in lessons.

Students get one chance; secondary school lasts from the age of 11 to the age of 16. We have that relatively short period of time in which to foster a love of sport and physical activity and give students the best chance of achieving excellent outcomes in PE. Let's not waste time. Let's ensure we provide a high-quality, evidence-informed educational experience for each and every student that we come across. As Marc Rowland says, 'Effective teaching is the best lever for improving school and pupil outcomes.'[1]

---

1 Rowland, *Addressing Educational Disadvantage in Schools and Colleges*, p. 65.

Bibliography

Allison, Shaun and Andy Tharby (2015). *Making Every Lesson Count: Six Principles to Support Great Teaching and Learning* (Carmarthen: Crown House Publishing).

Bandura, Albert (1977*).* Self-Efficacy: Toward a Unifying Theory of Behaviour Change, *Psychological Review,* 84(2): 191–215. Available at: https://educational-innovation.sydney.edu.au/news/pdfs/Bandura%20 1977.pdf.

Beck, Isabel L., Margaret G. McKeown and Linda Kucan (2002). *Bringing Words to Life: Robust Vocabulary Instruction* (New York: Guilford Press).

Boxer, Adam (2022). To Make Sure Your Students are Ready to Practise, Use Mini Whiteboards [video]. *Tips for Teachers* (10 March). Available at: https://www.youtube.com/watch?v=9OxEZRQu3NI.

Coe, Robert, Cesare Aloisi, Steve Higgins and Lee Elliot Major (2014). *What Makes Great Teaching? Review of the Underpinning Research* (London: Sutton Trust). Available at: https://www.suttontrust.com/ wp-content/uploads/2014/10/What-Makes-Great-Teaching-REPORT.pdf.

Cotton, Kathleen (1989). Classroom Questioning. Close-Up Number 5. *School Improvement Research Series III* (Portland, OR: Northwest Regional Educational Lab). Available at: https://educationnorthwest.org/sites/ default/files/ClassroomQuestioning.pdf.

Dunlosky, John (2013). Strengthening the Student Toolbox: Study Strategies to Boost Learning, *American Educator,* 37(3): 12–21. Available at: https://files.eric.ed.gov/fulltext/EJ1021069.pdf

Fletcher-Wood, Harry (2017). Guiding Student Improvement Without Individual Feedback, *Improving Teaching* [blog] (18 June). Available at: https://improvingteaching.co.uk/2017/06/18/guiding-student-improvement-without-individual-feedback/.

Hattie, John (2014). The Science of Learning. Keynote speech presented at Osiris World-Class Schools Convention, London.

Kahneman, Daniel (2011). *Thinking, Fast and Slow* (London: Allen Lane).

Kirby, Joe (2015). Knowledge Organisers, *Pragmatic Education* [blog] (28 March). Available at: https://pragmaticreform.wordpress.com/2015/03/ 28/knowledge-organisers/.

Lemov, Doug (2010). *Teach Like a Champion: 49 Techniques that Put Students on the Path to College* (San Francisco, CA: Jossey-Bass).

Lyman, Frank (1981). The Responsive Classroom Discussion. In A. S. Anderson (ed.), *Mainstreaming Digest* (College Park, MD: University of Maryland College of Education), pp. 109–113.

Miller, George A. (1956). The Magical Number Seven, Plus or Minus Two: Some Limits on Our Capacity for Processing Information, *Psychological Review*, 63(2): 81–97.

Muijs, Daniel and David Reynolds (2018). *Effective Teaching: Evidence and Practice*, 4th edn (London Sage).

Perry, Thomas, Rosanna Lea, Clara Rübner Jørgensen, Philippa Cordingley, Kimron Shapiro and Deborah Youdell (2021). *Cognitive Science Approaches in the Classroom: A Review of the Evidence* (London: Education Endowment Foundation). Available at: https://d2tic4wvo1iusb.cloudfront.net/production/documents/guidance/Cognitive_science_approaches_in_the_classroom_-_A_review_of_the_evidence.pdf?v=1690364866.

Perry, Thomas, Rosanna Lea, Clara Rübner Jørgensen, Philippa Cordingley, Kimron Shapiro and Deborah Youdell (2021). *Cognitive Science in the Classroom: Evidence and Practice Review* (London: Education Endowment Foundation). Available at: https://d2tic4wvo1iusb.cloudfront.net/production/documents/guidance/Cognitive_Science_in_the_classroom_-_Evidence_and_practice_review.pdf?v=1706001108.

Rosenshine, Barak (2012). Principles of Instruction: Research-Based Strategies That All Teachers Should Know, *American Educator*, 38(1): 12–19, 39. Available at: https://www.aft.org/sites/default/files/periodicals/Rosenshine.pdf.

Rowland, Marc (ed.) (2021). *Addressing Educational Disadvantage in Schools and Colleges: The Essex Way* (Woodbridge: John Catt).

Sherrington, Tom and Sara Stafford (2018). Questioning Techniques: 7. Pause-Pose-Pounce-Bounce (Chartered College of Teaching). Available at: https://my.chartered.college/wp-content/uploads/2018/10/7.-Pose-Pause-Pounce-Bounce-1.pdf.

Sweller, John (1994). Cognitive Load Theory, Learning Difficulty, and Instructional Design, *Learning and Instruction*, 4(4): 295–312. Available at: https://www.sciencedirect.com/science/article/abs/pii/0959475294900035.

Wiliam, Dylan (2011). *Embedded Formative Assessment* (Bloomington, IN: Solution Tree Press).

Wiliam, Dylan (2014). The Formative Evaluation of Teaching Performance. Centre for Strategic Education Occasional Paper 137 (September). Available at: https://www.dylanwiliam.org/Dylan_Wiliams_website/Publications_files/The%20formative%20evaluation%20of%20teaching%20performance%20%28CSE%202014%29%20secure.pdf.

Wiliam, Dylan (2016). The Secret of Effective Feedback, *Educational Leadership*, 73(7). Available at: https://www.ascd.org/el/articles/the-secret-of-effective-feedback.

Wiliam, Dylan and Paul Black (1990). *Inside the Black Box: Raising Standards Through Classroom Assessment* (London: GL Assessment).

Willingham, Daniel T. (2008–2009). What Will Improve a Student's Memory? *American Educator* (winter): 17–25. Available at: http://www.aft.org/sited/default/files/periodicals/willingham_0.pdf.

Willingham, Daniel T. (2010). *Why Don't Students Like School? A Cognitive Scientist Answers Questions About How the Mind Works and What It Means for the Classroom* (San Francisco, CA: Jossey-Bass).

Making Every Science Lesson Count

Six principles to support great science teaching

Shaun Allison

ISBN: 978-178583182-9

Making Every Science Lesson Count goes in search of answers to the fundamental question that all science teachers must ask: 'What can I do to help my students become the scientists of the future?'

Shaun points a sceptical finger at the fashions and myths that have pervaded science teaching over the past decade or so and presents a range of tools and techniques that will help science teachers make abstract ideas more concrete and practical demonstrations more meaningful.

Making Every MFL Lesson Count

Six principles to support great foreign language teaching

James A. Maxwell

ISBN: 978-178583396-0

Making Every MFL Lesson Count equips modern foreign language (MFL) teachers with practical techniques designed to enhance their students' linguistic awareness and to help them transfer the target language into long-term memory.

Written for new and experienced practitioners alike, *Making Every MFL Lesson Count* skilfully marries evidence-based practice with collective experience and, in doing so, inspires a challenging approach to secondary school MFL teaching.

Making Every Primary Lesson Count

Six principles to support great teaching and learning

Jo Payne and Mel Scott

ISBN: 978-178583181-2

Shares a host of strategies designed to cultivate a growth mindset in the primary school classroom and guide children towards independence: motivating both teachers and pupils to aim high and put in the effort required to be successful in all subject areas.

Jo and Mel also offer tips on how to implement effective routines and procedures so that students are clear about what is expected from them.

Making Every Maths Lesson Count

Six principles to support great maths teaching

Emma McCrea

ISBN: 978-178583332-8

Making Every Maths Lesson Count provides practical solutions to perennial problems and inspires a rich, challenging and evidence-based approach to secondary school maths teaching.

Emma shares gimmick-free advice that combines the time-honoured wisdom of excellent maths teachers with the most useful evidence from cognitive science – enabling educators to improve their students' conceptual understanding of maths over time.

Making Every History Lesson Count

Six principles to support great history teaching

Chris Runeckles

ISBN: 978-178583336-6

Writing in the practical, engaging style of the award-winning *Making Every Lesson Count*, Chris Runeckles articulates the fundamentals of great history teaching and shares simple, realistic strategies designed to deliver memorable lessons.

The book is underpinned by six pedagogical principles – challenge, explanation, modelling, practice, feedback and questioning – and equips history teachers with the tools and techniques to help students better engage with the subject matter and develop more sophisticated historical analysis and arguments.

Making Every Geography Lesson Count

Six principles to support great geography teaching

Mark Enser

ISBN: 978-178583339-7

Maps out the key elements of effective geography teaching to help teachers ensure that their students leave their lessons with an improved knowledge of the world, a better understanding of how it works and the geographical skills to support their understanding.

Mark offers an inspiring alternative to restrictive Ofsted-driven definitions of great teaching, and empowers geography teachers to deliver great lessons and celebrate high-quality practice.

Making Every English Lesson Count

Six principles to support great reading and writing

Andy Tharby

ISBN: 978-178583179-9

Making Every English Lesson Count is for new and experienced English teachers alike. It does not pretend to be a magic bullet. It does not claim to have all the answers. Rather the aim of the book is to provide effective strategies designed to help you to bring the six principles to life.

In an age of educational quick fixes, GCSE reform and ever-moving goalposts, this precise and timely addition to the Making Every Lesson Count series provides practical solutions to perennial problems and inspires a rich, challenging and evidence-informed approach to English teaching.

Making Every RE Lesson Count

Six principles to support religious education teaching

Louise Hutton and Dawn Cox

ISBN: 978-178583518-6

Writing in the practical, engaging style of the award-winning *Making Every Lesson Count*, Louise and Dawn provide teachers of religious education with the means to help their pupils unpick the big questions of religious belief and practice, and of morality and philosophy – the things that make us human.

Written for new and experienced practitioners alike, *Making Every RE Lesson Count* will enable teachers to improve their students' conceptual and contextual understanding of the topics and themes explored across the breadth of the RE curriculum.

Making Every Lesson Count

Six principles to support
great teaching and learning

Shaun Allison and Andy Tharby

ISBN: 978-184590973-4

This award-winning title has now inspired a whole series of books. Each of the books in the series are held together by six pedagogical principles – challenge, explanation, modelling, practice, feedback and questioning – and provide simple, realistic strategies that teachers can use to develop the teaching and learning in their classrooms.

A toolkit of techniques that teachers can use every lesson to make that lesson count. No gimmicky teaching – just high-impact and focused teaching that results in great learning, every lesson, every day.

Suitable for all teachers – including trainee teachers, ECTs (early career teachers) and experienced teachers – who want quick and easy ways to enhance their practice.

ERA Educational Book Award winner 2016. Judges' comments: 'A highly practical and interesting resource with loads of information and uses to support and inspire teachers of all levels of experience. An essential staffroom book.'